By *BarlowGirl* with *Andrew Barlow*

FOREWORD BY DEBORAH EVANS PRICE

Published in Nashville, Tennessee, by Word Books, A Division of Word Entertainment, LLC., A Warner/Curb Company. 25 Music Square West, Nashville, TN 37203.

ISBN: 1-933876-01-8

Printed in the United States of America

06 07 08 09 / 4 3 2 1

TABLE OF CONTENTS

BarlowGirl: The Followup

BarlowGirl: The Future

FOREWORD

For many people it takes nearly a lifetime to develop the courage to stand up for what they believe in. For Alyssa, Becca and Lauren Barlow that conviction seems as natural as breathing. Through their music and the way they live their lives, the young women of BarlowGirl beautifully share their faith and values with a hungry world.

As the parent of a teenage son, I'm grateful for music we can both listen to and enjoy. Any parent who has ever battled for control of the radio/CD player in their mini-van will tell you, it's great to find music that crosses generational boundaries and speaks to the heart in a musically relevant, yet lyrically potent way. BarlowGirl does that. They have an obvious army of teen fans, but there are a lot of us soccer moms who like to rock out too. BarlowGirl's music is totally entertaining, but it's also so much more.

I truly appreciate artists who take their platform seriously and are positive role models for today's youth, and I have tremendous respect for Alyssa, Becca and Lauren Barlow. Their stance on abstinence and sexual purity may not be something the world at large understands. After all, most teenagers can't wait to date, so to find three attractive girls in their 20s who don't believe in dating is unfathomable to some people. But the BarlowGirls know what they believe and why they believe it and aren't afraid to share those convictions with the world in their music, interviews and personal appearances.

To say they are great role models is an understatement. Their obedience to God and passion for sharing the gospel is impacting a generation. However, to get a teenager's attention, you have to earn their respect and Alyssa, Becca and Lauren Barlow first accomplished that with their music. Their songwriting and musicianship has earned them the appreciation of a legion of fans and the respect of an industry that can sometimes be skeptical when it comes to girl bands. One listen to BarlowGirl and any preconceived notions dissolve. These girls rock!

I've had the pleasure of interviewing BarlowGirl in my capacity as Christian music editor for Billboard magazine and they quickly became one of my favorite groups. I consider it an honor to be writing the forward for this delightful book. In reading it, I got to know them even better and you will too. As the title says, BarlowGirl is more than music. This book takes you behind the scenes into how God led them into music ministry, their individual struggles and triumphs, their relationship with their marvelous parents, and their life today—both on stage and off. In reading it, I laughed and I cried.

It's a wonderful glimpse into the lives of three very talented musicians using their gifts for God's glory. Rock on girls!

–Deborah Evans Price

BarlowGirl:
The Story

DECIDING TO JUMP

We've never been skydiving, but we think we know what it's like to stand in the doorway of a little airplane, deafened by the roar of the wind, looking down at the checkerboard earth below, with a decision to make. Jump or sit down? Trust the person who packed the parachute or land with the plane? Our moment of decision happened onstage at a little thing called the 2005 Dove Awards. Standing in front of thousands of the biggest names in the music industry (well, Lauren was actually sitting, but we digress), with those big TV cameras recording our every move, a string section waiting for our cue, we had a problem.

A big chain reaction of technical glitches basically left us deaf. We couldn't hear anything in our earpieces, not even our own voices. For girls who harmonize in pretty much every song we do, that's a problem. But, the clock was ticking and people were waiting so we had to make a call. Do we jump—start singing and risk sounding like those cats you hear in the backyard at night? Or sit back down and say "No go" and let people think we were just another cookie-cutter band that doesn't have what it takes? We had two advantages. Number one, we'd seen enough movie musicals to know the show must go on. Secondly, we knew God had brought us this far and would stay with us even if we sounded terrible. So we jumped.

The night before the Doves, we had shown up early for our 45-minute soundcheck, wanting to show we were legit professionals. We soundcheck all the time, so we knew we'd cruise right through, maybe even finish early. As soon as we started checking, though, we could tell something was wrong. Sound levels were all weird and the nervousness we'd been keeping under control was starting to make us sweat. Finally, after taking almost double our allotted time, we reached a point where the sound was finally good enough.

The sound engineer hit the "save" button on his console and we headed back to our hotel.

Showing up at the Doves the next day was a surreal experience. Here we were, three sisters from the Midwest, seeing and actually talking to artists we'd listened to our whole lives. Cameras were flashing. People were greeting each other with hugs. The production staff was shuttling people around. It was crazy. As we started rolling with our pre-show soundcheck, we looked over at the sound board and saw a group of people with concerned looks on their faces. Turns out the mix we'd all slaved over the night before had just disappeared. So, we spent the next twenty minutes rebuilding the mix then left the stage totally freaked out. The big cookbook of life was officially turned to the recipe for disaster.

Once the award show got rolling, we stood backstage watching the presenters' witty banter, listening to other acts perform and getting more nervous (the rickety little airplane was climbing...) At our cue, we hit the stage and plugged in, ready to rock. Unfortunately, Alyssa's earpieces weren't working, Lauren could literally hear an air traffic controller in hers and they couldn't hear Becca's guitar in the audience. It was not good. So, what'd we do? We did our version of standing up in the airplane, walking to the door, and not even looking before you jump. We looked at each other and shrugged. Alyssa pulled out her earbuds as she walked to the front of the stage and we kicked it.

We couldn't hear ourselves as we ripped through the song, but we felt really peaceful—definitely a God thing. As we finished and enjoyed the audience's reaction, we felt hugely relieved. "It's over," we thought. "Now we can get out of here." Well, we thought wrong.

The producer stepped onstage, quieted the crowd and announced that there were too many technical difficulties to use that song on the broadcast. We had to play it again. [Turns out our first parachute hadn't opened. Time to reach for that emergency chute.]

For just a second, we felt a twinge of nerves. It's one thing to perform in front of the biggest names on either side of the

Christian music microphone; it's another entirely to do it twice with absolutely no confidence in the sound system. [But, when you're free-fallin' you either grab the next ripcord or you don't. We grabbed the ripcord.] We did yet another quick soundcheck then, at the producer's cue, launched into our song again. As we started playing and singing, any nervousness we'd felt drained away—God was right there with us. When we finished, the audience reacted even better than they had the first time. Getting a standing ovation from people we'd always admired and listened to—Michael W. Smith, tobyMac, you name it—was a sweet way to finish up.

Like He has so many times in our life (and hopefully, keeps doing), God took us somewhere we couldn't have imagined being—places we could never earn on our merit—and stuck with us, showing us that He is the reason we do what we do. In His care, we arrived safely at the parachute landing zone, surrounded by industry well-wishers who now knew we weren't some thrown-together girl band with no skills. Once again, God reminded us that He is entirely trustworthy. He has given us our lives, our family and our music. So we want to glorify Him with everything we do, and every time He opens that door on the creaky little airplane of life, we just gotta jump.

SO, WHERE DID IT ALL START?

You could say that we BarlowGirls came by two things, our faith and our love for music, pretty honestly. Our parents met and fell in love in college right around the time the automobile was invented. (Ahem. Just kidding and checking to see if you're paying attention.) All his life, Dad had been a performer, singing and playing guitar wherever he could. He even opened for Harry Chapin one time. (Ask your parents who that is), and recorded his own album (which is like a CD but it's the size of a giant frisbee and shatters if you try to use it as one). He and Mom both had really strong relationships with Christ and were active in campus ministries. After they were married, they had a lot of the usual newlywed struggles like no money, no job, that sort of thing. But Dad really felt a call to the ministry, so they worked together to put him through graduate school, raised our brother together, and realized God was the only way to get through life.

Our dad served in a couple different ministries as the rest of us were born. He finally landed on staff at Willow Creek, the Chicago-area church we grew up in. As the worship leader in Promiseland, Willow's children's ministry, he found the perfect place to apply his musical talents and desire to serve Christ. At the time, there were some great things going on musically and creatively in "big church" but that was sort of just trickling down to kids' ministry. So, my dad started writing worship songs for kids that tied into the lessons we were learning. We can still remember him trying new songs out on us at home. If we liked them, he felt pretty sure the other kids would like them on Sunday morning.

At the same time, we were all learning to play piano. Our parents figured that was the best way to learn the basics of music. When we could play those 88 keys well enough to stop giving our listeners headaches, we were allowed to move onto the instruments we liked.

As our dad kept adding his songs to the worship he was leading at church, parents started asking for recordings of their own since their kids were singing them at home. With the church's backing he started recording his songs, cranking out five total CDs. When he decided he needed some kids' voices on the tracks, he trooped us over to the studio and plopped us in front of a microphone. We're sure he picked us because he has a great ear for vocal talent, not just because we were the first kids he saw.

The CDs were a hit with Willow families and started to spread around to other churches around the country. There were a lot of other children's ministers that were looking for fresh ideas and his CDs were a great fit. After listening to his songs, those ministers started calling, asking our dad about his philosophy on kid's worship, etc. Before long, he was getting invitations to lead worship at conferences and family retreats. As he started traveling, he felt weird teaching people about family togetherness while his family was miles away. Plus, our dad was still encouraging us in our music, so he persuaded us to be his three-girl backing band. At that time, we were "just" the Barlow girls, but something big was starting.

THE PEOPLE THAT YOU MEET

Playing as our dad's backup band was great experience for us. Since his music was targeted at kids, our audiences were usually, well, little. If you've ever spent time with the whole birth-to-twelve crowd, you know they're easily distracted. You gotta work to keep their attention. So we learned to amp up our show so that our audience wouldn't lose interest and wander off. (When you see us jumping around onstage and hear us talking between songs at our concerts, you're seeing some of the habits we developed in those early days.) We loved playing at church family camps and conferences. We got great experience, met amazing people and had tons of chances to worship God with our music. After more than a year of playing church events, our dad started getting calls from festival promoters.

In the Christian music world, summertime is festival season. Students are out of school looking for something to do, families are on vacation and the weather is better for outdoor shows. There are festivals all over the place, so a band can play almost every weekend if they build their schedule right. We weren't invited to the big stages right away. We started playing on the smaller stages that festivals offer to reach a wider range of people. After performing for family audiences in the kids' area, we'd head over to the main stage area to see the other bands.

Each festival season, a core group of bands usually develops and travels like a caravan of nomads from event to event. They get to know each other pretty well from sharing gear, watching each other perform, and waiting around backstage. At LifeFest '99 in Oshkosh, Wisconsin, we were in the backstage catering area looking for lunch when our dad ran into a guy he knew from Willow Creek named Max Hsu. Max was the founder and leader of Superchic[k], a band that was getting a lot of attention for their

killer sound, high energy and great message. We could tell it wasn't going to be a short conversation between those two, so we grabbed our food, plopped down with the rest of Superchic[k] and struck up a conversation.

As we ate and talked, somebody from Superchic[k] noticed the rings on our left hands and mentioned we looked a little young to be married. We clued them in that our jewelry was purity rings that our parents had given us as a reminder of our decision to not date. They seemed fascinated by the concept, so we had a chance to share our perspective on not dating. It was a great conversation that blossomed into friendship over the next few festivals.

Not too long after that first meeting at LifeFest, the band invited us to one of their Chicago-area concerts then asked us to come over to Max's house afterwards. When we got there, they said they had a surprise for us and made us sit down. Someone pressed play on the stereo and one of the cuts from their upcoming CD started pouring out of the speakers. When we heard the opening chords, we were impressed—very energetic and cool with the scratching turntable sounds. But then the words started and our jaws dropped—it was about us.

As we listened to "Barlow Girls" we were absolutely floored—it's a weird feeling to hear someone sing a nice song about you. Plus, we'd been feeling a little beat up by criticism we'd been getting about our stance on dating. Their friendship would have been enough, but writing an incredible song about us really made us feel good. It was a gift that God knew we needed. We pretty much kept it under control as we listened to the rest of the song and thanked our new friends as we left. We may have been cool inside, but we lost it when we got to the car. When the doors closed and we were alone, we paused, looked at each other then screamed our heads off in amazement, excitement, shock and more excitement. It was crazy.

"Barlow Girls" was one of the biggest singles from their album, Karaoke Superstars. As it played more and more on radios, people started clueing into the concept of no dating,

staying pure, all that. A supportive web site even sprang up and we started to hear stories of teens who were starting to call themselves BarlowGirls as a sign of their own decision for purity. It was kind of weird to hear that at first, but that feeling was soon replaced by joy at what God was doing through a vision he'd placed on our family's heart long ago.

It's been a couple of years since we first heard the song, but it continues to inspire us. Any time we're feeling lonely or let down or start to think this whole thing is not worth it, we can pop in that song and get a fresh burst of inspiration and energy. It helps us to keep pushing on who God has called us to be.

THE ULTIMATE RELATIONSHIP

We come from a really big family. Our Mom is one of 10 kids and Dad has 13 brothers and sisters—we have almost 40 cousins just on Dad's side of the family tree. In a family as big as ours, you get to go to a lot of weddings. One of the best parts of those get-togethers is hearing the story of how the couple met, how they knew they had found "the one" for them. We each have our own relationship story like that, but they're about finding "the one" who matters most: God. Of course, someday we'll have a story to tell about how we met our own husbands, but as we say in our song, "Average Girl," we're "just waiting."

Growing up with a dad who was in ministry and a mom who prays like most people breathe, we were pretty much aware of God from the get-go. Not only did we hear about God at church, but He was part of our life at home—everything from prayers before meals and bedtime to the subject of our family devotional times. Our parents were very deliberate about letting us know who Jesus is and about his promise of salvation. So, all three of us had confessed our belief in Him before we were 10-years-old. It was the relational part that took a little longer.

Becca's story: I pretty much grew up the shyest girl on the planet. I don't know why, but I avoided attention at every turn, mostly because I felt I didn't deserve it. My goal in any social situation was to disappear as quickly as possible. I worked hard to be the "good girl," but, even when I succeeded at stuff, felt like I'd failed. In that period between finishing high school and preparing for college, things came to a head—my doubts about my physical appearance had led me down the road into a full-blown eating disorder and depression had started to creep into my life. It was a dark time that found me on the floor of our bathroom at home, empty

emotionally, spiritually and physically. I cried out in my heart to God—sure, I'd signed on his dotted line when I was younger, but, at that moment, I needed more than a ticket to heaven. I genuinely needed a personal relationship with a savior who could heal me.

In that moment, I honestly heard Him speaking to me for the first time. I heard Him gently telling me that I'd been destroying my body, ruining the temple he'd created to be beautiful, but that He loved me no matter what. In an instant, He changed the way I viewed myself. It was like a veil falling away from my eyes, allowing me to see what I'd been doing and how I hated what He created—me. Overwhelmed by His unconditional love, I decided on the spot that He is a God that I would love to serve for the rest of my life. We captured that moment of insight in our song, "Mirror," proclaiming our commitment to seeing ourselves through God's eyes, not the world.

Alyssa: Between the ages of four and eight, I probably prayed to accept Christ about once a week. I just had this fear that Jesus either didn't hear me the last time I prayed or that He took off every time I made a mistake. My parents certainly never taught me that, I just pieced that together myself. I spent my time working as hard as I could doing God-ish things, making sure He noticed my commitment. Truth is, He had my works, He had my thoughts, but He never really had my heart or my genuine surrender.

When I was 18, an ankle injury escalated into RSD, a debilitating over-reaction of the nervous system to pain. Stuck in my bedroom for what seemed like an eternity, I got angry with God. He'd given me gifts and talents I was sure were going to carry me to the Broadway stage and now I was stuck in bed, unable to prove how much I deserved His love. Over those several months, as He healed me from RSD, I finally gave in, telling Him, "I'm Yours. I'm gonna live for You, not just in the hard work sense. The rest of my life, I'm gonna spend my days in love with You, following You no matter what my own plans are." In the end (not that we've ended anything—I'm only in my twenties), that's what my relationship with Him is about.

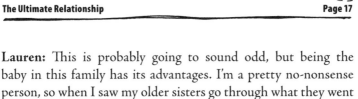

Lauren: This is probably going to sound odd, but being the baby in this family has its advantages. I'm a pretty no-nonsense person, so when I saw my older sisters go through what they went through, I told God, "I'm in. You loving me and my loving You back is the only way to go." I wish I could share something more dramatic than that, but that's my deal. I just try to start every day by refocusing on my commitment to God and living for him.

ROCKY MOUNTAIN BREAKTHROUGH

A lot of people think performing onstage is a unique, fantasy-like experience, completely disconnected from reality. If you ask us, it's really just everyday life magnified a thousand times. Like everyday life, things go wrong all the time: equipment fails, you forget your words or sing a wrong note. And all those things happen in plain sight of people who are quick to judge and critique. Like everyday life, you'll do a lot better onstage if you can laugh at your own mistakes and keep rolling. Most of all, you'll be most fulfilled in either arena if you're doing what you love to do, what God created you to do. We learned that lesson big time during the Music in the Rockies seminar in 2002.

Between the 1999 and 2000 LifeFests, we started our move from backing up our dad to being our own band. In 2001, we responded to God's gentle leading and set aside the children's music thing to pursue our own band. In what we still consider an amazing act of sacrifice, our Dad stepped into the background to support what we wanted to do: performing as BarlowGirl. As we played on our own more and more, we realized that we needed some training to take us to the next level.

We were praying and keeping our eyes open for instruction opportunities when our mom heard an ad on the radio talking about Music in the Rockies. We'd never heard of it, but the Gospel Music Association puts on an annual training session in Estes Park, Colorado for aspiring bands and singers. This sounded like just the thing for us, but our excitement died down a little when we started adding up what it would cost to get out there for a week. We prayed hard about it, asking God to get us there if it was His plan. Like He has done a million times already, God handled it. Some friends of our family heard us talking about the seminar and told us they'd fund the whole trip. (God is cool like that.) So

we headed to Colorado.

When we got there, we found out two interesting things. One, the seminar wasn't just about training—it was more about bands getting onstage and "learning while doing" under the watchful eyes of music industry executives. Second, we confirmed a suspicion of ours that the rock band life is mostly a guy thing—all-girl bands are more the exception than the rule. When we showed up the first day, we found out that we'd be performing and competing as the only all-girl band out of like 30 acts. (Competing? What is that about? We just like to play for people.) But, God had brought us that far, we decided we were gonna show 'em what we had.

The first time we stepped onstage, we were way nervous. We were looking at a row of judges sitting there American Idol-style and an audience full of our competition. We were positive it was going to be brutal, so we just threw caution to the wind and rocked out the way we love to play. We weren't even halfway done with our first song when we saw some guys in the audience standing up and rocking along with us. Their enthusiasm relaxed us, so we played harder. When we finished, the judges gave us great feedback and a pass into the next round.

The second round performance was even more stressful—one of the judges that day was a bonafide celebrity, Michael Tait of dcTalk—but we weren't going to back down. Adding to our stress, Lauren had gotten a bad case of altitude sickness, so she was now alternating looking green and lying around like a dead person with--how shall we put this delicately--barfing a lot. When we were called to take the stage, we told Lauren she could finish barfing later and headed out to play. We plugged in and smiled at the judges as we waited for Lauren's usually rock-steady 1-2-3-4 countdown. For some reason, she stopped after three, so we started on the wrong beat and totally train-wrecked the song. As we stumbled through the intro, we looked back at Lauren to find out what her problem was and saw her playing one-handed. Turns out her other drumstick had gotten caught in her pigtail during the countdown and was stuck there, no matter how hard she pulled.

As much as we wanted to just stop and laugh our heads off, we couldn't—as you know, the show must go on. So we kept playing while Lauren tried to dislodge the stick from her hair. Even though it had roughed up the start of the song, her little mishap had completely blown away any tension in the room and allowed us to play even more freely than the day before. Before we knew it, we were done and the judges, including Michael Tait, advanced us to the finals.

It'd be great to say that we won the battle-of-the-bands that week, but we didn't. Instead, we won what we consider a bigger victory: God got us the training we'd asked for and shown us that we could hang with the boys onstage. We also met some people in the music industry who saw our potential and would eventually help our career. As we headed home and the Rocky Mountains got smaller and smaller in our rear-view mirror, we had that sense of peace you get when you're doing what God has created and called you to do. And a great sense of curiosity about what He had in store for us next. Little did we know that it would be a giant game of leapfrog.

A GIANT GAME OF LEAPFROG

The time between Music in the Rockies and going into the studio to record our first CD really was like a giant, yearlong game of leapfrog. If the bank of the pond was our comfortable life at home, the first lily pad was a professional relationship that started with a guy we met in Colorado whose job was finding new talent for a huge Christian record label. After watching our performances, he approached us with the offer of a development deal. (How's that for fancy music business talk?) Things were on a roll and we felt like God had thrown open a huge door for us. So we were surprised and seriously bummed a couple months later when we learned that a) our contact quit his job at the label and b) his replacement didn't know about us.

We kept turning to God for guidance and patience and kept hearing from Him that music was still His plan for us. So, we persisted in practicing and writing and praying a whole lot. After a while, another contact in the industry asked us to try out, so we put on our own mini-concert in a church basement. He liked our sound and invited us to Nashville where he handled all the arrangements for recording our first demo, including renting a studio and lining up the producer. One of the best things that came out of that session was meeting the producer, the amazing Otto Price, who took us under his wing and kept us moving in God's direction.

In his shy, meek, quiet way (if you knew Otto, you'd know none of those words apply, but more on that in the next chapter) Otto started introducing us to people he knew, including Susan Riley, the founder of Fervent Records. We first met Susan over lunch where we all hit it off on a personal level. She seemed to connect with what we were about in terms of our life choices and our vision for our music. She said she'd heard our demo and wanted us to

play live for her and the other executives at her company. So we set up yet another mini-concert (or "showcase" in music business speak) this time at Otto's church and did our thing yet again.

The day after our showcase, Susan and her husband asked us to meet them at a coffee shop where they offered us a recording contract. It was an amazing moment, but we had learned not to leap right away at anything—and we didn't want to seem too eager—so we thanked them and asked for time to think and pray about it as a family.

It didn't take us long to decide. As we prayed and reflected on the vision God had given us for our music, what our experiences had taught us, and what we knew about Susan and her team, it ended up being an easy decision. God had put us into position for this next jump, so we pretty much joined hands as a family and followed his leading. We signed on the dotted line with Fervent Records and immediately started work on our first CD. Our little game of leapfrog had been both stressful and educational, but with God's help, we'd won.

WE'VE SEEN AN ANGEL

Most people who draw pictures of angels dress them in robes with feathery white wings and a harp. Our angel is a large black man with a bass guitar in his hand, a permanent smile on his face and a cell phone apparently welded to his ear. Otto Price is a walking, talking, living, breathing angel sent straight from God into our lives.

We first met him in May 2003 when we'd been invited to Nashville to record a demo. Apparently Otto owed a favor to the guy who was helping us, so he agreed, after some eye rolling ("A girl band? You can't be serious…") to oversee a brief studio session. Since he doesn't like to go into the studio cold, he set up a meeting the night before our session in, of all places, a Wal-Mart parking lot.

So here we were, three girls and our parents (they keep a good eye on us) sitting around on our car after dark waiting to meet some stranger named Otter or Auto or something. As we were nervously chatting, a sweet Bronco rolled up, driven by a man talking excitedly on his cell phone (a picture we would see thousands of times again—he is one connected man). In an instant we recognized him as the bassist for SonicFlood and dcTalk—a genuine, amazing celebrity coming to meet us. He finished his call then, bang, he flipped his phone shut, bounded out of his car and hugged all of us; an explosion of energy and love and friendship. Right there on the spot, we prayed together then started talking a mile a minute, often all at the same time, like we'd known each other forever. We knew in an instant that this was our guy and that we'd sell a kidney (probably Lauren's—she's the youngest) to have him as our producer.

Since that time, Otto has been our champion. For years, we'd prayed for someone who would lovingly help us take our music to

the next level and navigate the maze that is the music business. He's that guy. In the true scriptural sense, he rejoices with us when we rejoice, he weeps with us when we weep. Sometimes he just weeps and laughs for no reason. He is more honest with his emotions than just about any guy we know.   He is the guy who convinced Alyssa that it's okay to be a bass player, scheduled Lauren's first drum lesson, and challenges Becca to attempt tougher solos with every song.

Because he so clearly loves us and wants the best for us, he's really the one person who can truly push us in the studio. He knows just how much we can take (and, yes, there have been tears in the studio) and when to break the tension. Picture him blasting a Shania Twain song and leading us in a dance around the studio and you'll know he'd do just about anything to help us do our best. He is definitely our brother from another mother, a man we dearly love who has helped us along the path to where we are now and, we hope, will help us continue our growth as artists and Christ-followers. What can we say? He's our angel.

CRACK THAT WHIP

Lauren: Have you ever found yourself standing in the backyard of the drummer from an all-girl 80's heavy metal band, trying to make a bullwhip crack and said to yourself, "How on earth did I get here?" Well, I have and it's a weird experience. In 2003, we were in the recording studio working on our first CD when I came face-to-face with my own limitations.

I don't learn the way most kids do, so I've spent my life teaching myself stuff at my own pace, including the drums. I never had a lesson before I went onstage as a drummer—I just picked up the sticks and started banging away, going with the rhythms and combinations I felt. That approach served me pretty well. It got me through the first couple years of playing onstage at churches and music festivals. I played with enough energy, creativity and attitude that my level of technical skill didn't completely matter. However, when we got into the studio, there was nowhere to hide.

Life in the recording studio might sound glamorous, but it's hard work. And, the hardest part for me is the fact that you need to do a song the exact same way over and over until it's just right. Then you make a tiny tweak and do it the new way exactly right ten more times in a row. When Otto, our producer, would recommend a different approach, or change a structure, I struggled a little to keep up. Each take of each song made me feel a little worse—I felt like I was holding us back. That nagging voice in the back of my mind kept telling me I was going to ruin everything for my family because I wasn't learning quickly enough, that my lack of formal training made me the weak link in our band. So, I finally lost it.

I was talking to Otto during a lunch break when I just started to cry. We were talking about how hard drumming can be and the frustration I'd been feeling just boiled over. To make it worse, I was the first sister to cry in the studio. (I'm supposed to be the tough

one cuz I'm the drummer.) When we first entered the studio, we'd lifted a line from the movie, A League of Their Own, and made it ours. Whenever things got especially tough, we'd tell each other "There's no crying in rock & roll!" That was usually enough to break the tension and keep us going. This time it didn't help—the tears came in a flood. Any guy in that situation would probably be a little puzzled. I'm guessing that Otto, whose kids were all boys at that time, probably hadn't dealt with too many weepy girls, but to his credit, he was just himself and stuck with me.

As he listened to me cry, Otto kept talking in that sweet voice of his, saying things like, "It's all right, you're doing great, It's gonna be fine." Finally, either because I felt better or I got dehydrated and ran out of tears, I stopped crying. Otto looked at me as I wiped my eyes—I think my lunch was swimming in mascara at that point—and said, "If you're that worried about not being trained, let's get you a lesson. We're going to get you a lesson right now."

So, he dialed his cell phone and called a woman who had been a drummer in an all-girl rock band years before I was born. She had some time available, so I headed to her house as quickly as I could for my emergency lesson. She set me up on her drum set and watched me play for a while. She could tell that my stick grip and the way I attacked the drums was going to cause me trouble in the long term (I'd already been having some tendonitis in my wrists, but just figured it was the cost of rockin'.) So, she disappeared into another room for a second and returned with a bullwhip in her hand. At first, I was worried that she was going to use it to "encourage" me to play better, but instead she told me to follow her into the backyard. There, she explained to me that I needed to snap my wrist when I played, just like cracking a whip.

So, I stood there for almost a half hour, wondering the whole time what her neighbors must be thinking, trying to crack the whip without taking my eye out. I finally took a minute to pray, asking God to help me with this. Then on what was probably the millionth attempt, it happened. CRACK. Then I did it again and again. I felt like Indiana Jones without the hat. I couldn't wait to get back to her drum set. I sat down and started "cracking the whip"

on the cymbals and drums and instantly felt better. I thanked my first drum teacher and headed out the door, ready to get back into the studio.

It's funny that God let me go as far as I could with something, waiting patiently until I turned to Him and accepted help from the people He'd put in my life. Those moments of brokenness and surrender to Him are the way He genuinely changes us and moves us forward on his plan for our lives. Being a bit hard-headed, it sometimes takes me longer to let go, but He has never disappointed me when I do. So, if you ever have one of those standing-in-the-backyard-of-an-80s-all-girl-rock-band-cracking-a-whip-moments, remember that God has you there for a reason.

LETTING BABY OUT THE DOOR

When you were growing up, do you remember those times like Easter church or weddings when you had to look your best? We remember how our mom would line us up in the hallway before we left the house to make sure we were ready to go. She would straighten our clothes, check our hair, then look us in the eye one last time with a reminder of how to behave. She would cover everything from how to shake a grown-up's hand to the rules for safely crossing the street. Then, when we passed the visual inspection and verbal quiz, we were ready to head out into the world. To be honest, we didn't love that process when we were kids, but, now that we've released a CD, we have a much better understanding of it. Preparing a collection of songs for release is a nerve-wracking experience, a lot like letting your kid out the front door for the first time.

Like parents, we wanted our "offspring" to sound their best. Our songs almost always start small, as a line or two in a journal or a chord progression discovered during a long car ride. By the time they're burned onto a CD, they've "grown up" in the studio, sporting multiple instruments, layers of harmonies, and cool digital effects. By that time, we've heard them so many times that we can hardly tell if they're worth listening to anymore. But they better be good because we hope and pray that God will use our music to touch people's lives. So we pay close attention to "how they look" before we pat them on the head and say "Have a nice day."

The second stress in sending our "baby" out the door for the first time is that the world can be a big cruel place. You wouldn't want your kid to be picked on in school any more than we want our songs to be shredded by a music critic. We cherish our songs and admit that they're an extension of who we are. If they get bullied in the big schoolyard of life, those criticisms hurt us too. And we don't want

our "child" to be ignored either. God is our provider, so we can't worry about sales numbers, but there's that moment of hesitation before you swing that door open and let junior out to play when you wonder if the other kids will play nice.

One big difference between our hopes and those of a parent is that we definitely want our music to talk to strangers. We want people from every walk of life, every faith background, to get to know our "kids." We hope that our music can be a vehicle for people who don't know Jesus from a hole in the ground to discover the unending joy of a relationship with Him.

Whether you're a parent or an artist, the time always arrives when you use a little bit of spit to fix that last stray hair, plant a kiss on your little ones and watch as they head out the door. When we finished the recording and mastering process with our CD, we had no idea what to expect. As the release date of BarlowGirl approached, all we could do was trust that we'd done our best and leave the results up to Him.

BarlowGirl:
The Album

(BEHIND THE SONGS ON *BARLOWGIRL*)

ON MY OWN

Have you ever noticed that, of all the problems or weaknesses available in the world, you tend to slide backward into a certain few? Since God made everyone different, it makes sense that we'd each deal with different struggles. For as long as we can remember, we have fallen into the trap of comparing ourselves to each other, feeling jealous because we felt that one of us was thinner, or got more attention, or had nicer stuff, things like that. (If you have a brother or sister and you're an actual human being, you might have heard that siblings sometimes don't get along in ways that can be annoying to pretty much everyone within a one-mile radius.) It caused a ton of stress in our house. Our frequent squabbles drove us and our parents crazy. Our parents set up rules to cut down on the conflict, but we didn't make a lot of progress. Out of desperation, we all committed to start praying about it. Hard. So we talked about it, journaled about it, and prayed some more.

As we reflected on repeated slides into angry conflict, God showed us that backsliding is part of the human sin nature. How often have you said to yourself, "I should be over this by now," or "As a Christian, I have learned the right answers, so I should be changed," but not gotten any better? These failures can cause guilt to pile up which then keeps us from accepting love from God or anyone else. As we wrestled with this issue, we felt God saying "to whip an issue this big, you have to let Me change your heart. And change like this won't happen all at once—get ready for a process."

When you listen to "On My Own" we hope you'll realize you're not unusual if you don't work things out the first time you pray about them. We even toyed with calling the song "Thousandth Time" because that's how it feels when any of us mess up yet again. All we can do is encourage you to keep crying out to Him, the God who loves you, and ask Him to change your heart.

ON MY OWN

I can't believe that I'm here in this place again
How did I manage to mess up one more time?
This pattern seems to be the story of my life
Should have learned this lesson by the thousandth time

'Cause I promised myself I wouldn't fall
But here I've fallen
I guess I'm not as strong as I thought
All I can do is cry to You

Oh God You have to save me
You're my last and only hope
All my right answers fail me
I can't seem to make it on my own

I always thought that I would be strong enough
What made all of them fall couldn't take me down
Yeah, did I think that I was above it all
I have learned that pride comes before the fall

I can't promise myself that I won't fall
'Cause here I've fallen
I know I'm not as strong as I thought
All I can do is cry to You

PEDESTAL

We love movies. Ever since we were little, we would watch quality movies as a family and even now use them to wind down together after a busy day. Comedies and Broadway musicals are probably our favorites. A couple years ago we also had a favorite actor. He had been great in a bunch of great movies and seemed like a wonderful guy. Okay, we admit it; we thought he was cute, too. So, we kinda started to assume he was like his characters: smart, innocent, clever, possibly the perfect guy.

One day, a friend of ours who lives in New York City called with huge news: she had actually seen our fave actor in real life. "What was he like?" we shrieked. We couldn't wait to hear our assumptions about this great guy confirmed. Our friend was quiet for a second then let us down gently. "You would not be impressed," she said. "He was kinda being a jerk." We were crushed: How could this guy who was so sweet and charming on screen be less than perfect?

We'd like to tell you we reacted gracefully, but, in our minds, he instantly became the worst guy in the world. "If he does that stuff in public, I bet he's a total jerk in real life," we said. We really started ripping the guy. This guy was just another human being, but we'd put him on a pedestal, assuming things about him we didn't know. Then, when he acted like humans do, we not only knocked him off the pedestal (the one that we put him on in the first place!!), but also started kicking him when he was down.

In our prayer times, we approached God with the way we were feeling and, through His Word, began to understand a simple truth. He essentially said that our need to idolize was something He had put into each of us. He told us, "There is something you're designed to put on a pedestal and admire. That would be Me." Sadly, it's human nature to fill that spot on the pedestal with people. No matter how great they are, because they're not God,

they will inevitably let you down.

God's sense of humor shows through the fact that we, as BarlowGirl, encounter this more all the time. We get the saddest notes from people who are crushed because they disagreed with a choice we made. We try to remind people that, because we're human too, we'll disappoint them eventually. God is the only One who belongs on the pedestal of our life. Until we understand that, until we're keeping Him in the center of it all, we'll spend our days disappointed.

PEDESTAL

You're the coolest person
That I have ever seen
So perfect with your pretty face
On the TV screen

You're a god I know it
How you stand above them all
You are my perfect person
Man I'd hate to see you fall

I want someone to believe in
Yeah well don't we all?
'Cause in this life of imperfection
Need someone who won't fall
You got it, you got it, you got it all

Got a magazine today
That was full of you
Shocked to read the words they said
Tell me they're not true

Add you to my fallen list
One more has hit the ground

The fault was mine
Held you too high
Your only way was down

I can't deny this need inside
I have to find the perfect one
But I wonder if behind my need
There might just be a reason?

Is my life just one big searching
For the one I can adore?
It never works
And I'm just left here wanting more

Could it be this hunger is there
To drive me to the One
Who's worthy of all worship
Would my searching then be done?

NEVER ALONE

God works on people in the most amazing ways. For example, look at us—we have always liked music, but were way too shy and unsure of ourselves to even think about singing in public. God knew what He was doing, though. He patiently kept throwing challenges and opportunities at us until, before we realized it, we were playing, praying and thinking as a band. Reaching that point was plenty for us—we were comfortable with our situation and wanted to "keep it real" and reserve our music for ourselves. We pretty much gritted our teeth, clenched our spiritual fists and said, "We'll never sign with a label." Newsflash: God loves "never" statements.

Like He always does, He kept firmly nudging us, in this case with phone calls from different labels (a fancy name for a record company), encouragement from various people, and a growing joy in music. One day we heard from a guy who represented a big label, one that handled a lot of really well-known artists. When he told us his company was interested in us, we got excited. In our mind's eye, we instantly saw an entire recording career stretching out in front of us, picturing ourselves doing the whole "one earphone on, one off, singing with our eyes closed" look that you always see in videos. It was our time.

We quit our jobs. Becca and Alyssa dropped out of college and our parents started wrapping up the family counseling practice they'd been doing. We were ready to make it happen. About six months after that first conversation, our contact called to say he was leaving the label and, by the way, no one else there was really interested in us. In the blink of an eye, our dreams vaporized. Poof. We were "just another band" again.

That kicked off a really dark three-months for us. Jobless, too late to get back to school for the semester, mourning the death of the future we'd pictured, we were seriously bummed. For a couple

of months, we basically sat around the house with no direction, feeling like total losers. With nowhere else to turn, we leaned on each other and pressed into God. We got real honest with Him too, writing in our journals about our feelings of disappointment and abandonment. We asked Him. "Where did we miss you?" "Where are you?" "Why have you pulled your hand away from us?" It really hurt. But, over time, God really worked on our hearts until we could honestly say to Him, "We'll do whatever You want us to do, even if that means just writing songs that only we will hear."

One morning, we were in our living room praying and talking through our latest journal entries while Becca strummed idly on her guitar. We couldn't tell exactly what our parents were talking about in the next room, but their tone told us they were sad too. On an impulse, Alyssa flipped open her journal and found some phrases she'd written over and over and sang them to the melody Becca was playing. "I cried out and no reply, I can't feel you by my side" just flowed out. Instantly, our Dad appeared in the doorway and asked, "What was that song?" He asked us to sing it again so we did, as Lauren added a harmony. "You need to finish that song," our Dad said, so we spent the next forty minutes on it, words flying out of our hearts and onto the page. We'd never written a song that quickly. Ever.

Months later, after we'd finally signed with Fervent Records and entered the studio, our producer, the amazing Otto Price, insisted on hearing everything we'd ever written. We shared every single song but, when we got to this one, we just badmouthed it. "It only took us 45 minutes to write it." "The structure is weird—it needs rewriting." "It's too simple." Thankfully, Otto, Dad & Mom ignored our complaints and insisted we record it for the album.

When we hear stories of how Never Alone has impacted people, we're reminded of the work God did in our lives during that sad time. Although the song came together in under an hour, God was actually writing it in our hearts during the difficult months before that session. No matter how far away He felt from us, He was and is right there. We were never alone.

NEVER ALONE

I waited for you today
But You didn't show
No no no
I needed You today
So where did You go?
You told me to call
Said You'd be there
And though I haven't seen You
Are You still there?

I cried out with no reply
And I can't feel You by my side
So I'll hold tight to what I know
You're here and I'm never alone

And though I cannot see You
And I can't explain why
Such a deep, deep reassurance
You've placed in my life
We cannot separate
'Cause You're part of me
And though You're invisible
I'll trust the unseen

HARDER THAN THE FIRST TIME

Once we signed with Fervent Records, we had a lot of things to do before going into the recording studio. Besides paperwork and meetings, there was rehearsal time and one other teeny, tiny detail: making sure we had enough songs to fill an entire CD. We'd been writing songs for years and accumulated a nice library, but not all of them were "CD-worthy." After weeding out the not-quite-ready ones, we discovered we were one song short. We tried a couple of different approaches to writing this last one, but kept drawing a big fat blank. So, with just one week to go before we entered the studio, we decided to mix things up and headed off to a worship conference for some great teaching and amazing times of worship. Then, on our lunch breaks, we'd grab our notebooks and Becca's guitar and head for the pool, ready to work.

It turned out to be a big challenge. Nothing would come—we felt a little odd outside of our natural habitat—we'd always done our writing in our living room. We started to worry that our creative well had dried up a little. Then, during one of the teaching times, the speaker completely blew us away with his testimony. He was totally on fire for God. He had lived the first part of his life far from God and was so grateful for being saved that he practically glowed. Later, we sat with our toes in the water of the pool, wishing we were that on fire for God.

As pastor's kids, we'd learned about Jesus at an early age and, guided by our parents, lived within the white lines. As we talked and prayed by the pool, God revealed to us that, although we'd never strayed in a big, obvious way, we had drifted bit by bit, staging mini-rebellions in our hearts that left us feeling kind of spiritually numb. When we confessed that to God and acknowledging that sin in our own hearts, it was like something broke loose and Harder Than The First Time flowed out. (Yet again, God was using everything He can get His hands on to shape us.)

We hit the studio at full speed and recorded this song as part of our sessions. In the months that followed the release of our CD, we started hearing stories about Harder inspiring people to re-energize their relationship with God. It proved to us (and, yes, God needs to remind us of stuff FREQUENTLY) that He can use anything from a natural disaster to a song that flowed out of our own confession to touch people and bring about His will. He never stops amazing us.

HARDER THAN THE FIRST TIME

I walked with you
Just like we've done for so long
You seem so near
But even that's become so common
It's not just You, just been together so long
That I thought I knew everything about You
But today I saw
Did You open up my eyes?
'Cause I feel like I've just seen You for the first time

I didn't see You
But God I want to
You've come alive
And I think I've fallen harder than the first time

Was I so blind?
How did I not see You?
Yet in all that time You never left my side
So for all my life I will live to know You
So here I am, I'll take Your hand

I see Your face
I feel You close
The love You've always shown me
Won't miss it now can't waste a day
Jesus I'm Yours completely

YOU LED ME

After almost three months in the studio, we were beat. We had recorded and polished all but one of the songs for BarlowGirl, but needed a break before we could finish. We just wanted to sleep in our own beds, see our brother and his family, and take some time to recharge, so we piled into the car. During the nine-hour drive from Nashville to Chicago, we felt tired but amazed as we reflected on all that God had done over the past few months. As the mile markers sped by, we heard a chord progression taking shape in the back seat where Becca was noodling on her ever-present guitar. We told her, "You gotta keep that one."

A day or two later, the three of us were lounging in Alyssa's bedroom, enjoying that comfy home feeling, warming up in the morning light that pours through her windows on sunny days. As Becca started playing that chord progression from the car on her guitar, a picture began to form in Alyssa's head. The combination of the morning sunshine and Becca's beautiful music brought to mind a person stretching and yawning, greeting not only another day on the calendar, but also a new, fresh day in his or her relationship with God.

The thing that makes morning so great is that it chases away the darkness of night. We open our eyes to see that the scary shape in the corner of the bedroom is just a jacket and the thing scratching the window was a tree branch. Just like an actual night time, everyone has times in his or her life that are dark spiritually, relationally, emotionally. "You Led Me" describes one of those sweet moments when the tough times are giving way to new life and God's fresh opportunities are coming into view. And, as God's presence flares in our lives again, His love illuminates those things that were scaring us, showing them for what they are and reminding us that He was with us all along. The Bible and our own experiences teach us that a) even the most difficult moments

can be used for His purposes, b) tough times are part of being human and c) because He loves us, God never leaves us.

We wrote most of You Led Me in Alyssa's room that day, but it still wasn't done when we started our return trip to Nashville. We weren't worried though. We knew we could trust Him. For seven of the next nine hours, Becca sat in the back of the car and played until her hands ached. The payoff was great, though. Not only did God give us the ending of that song before we got to Nashville, we were able to write another complete song on the way. Even as Nashville and the studio got closer with every mile marker, we never freaked out. The knowledge that God had proven himself faithful a million times before gave us peace and the courage to trust him for what we needed.

YOU LED ME

Good Morning the night is over and gone
I thought once this dark would last for so long

Feel the sunlight on my face
You have brought me through this place

Jesus, Jesus You found me
Through the long night you led me
You set me free

Do you see just what You've done in my life?
You gave me more than I hoped for now I
Feel Your sunlight on my face
You have brought me through this place

MIRROR

Becca: Every room in our house is full of memories. Our living room calls to mind family prayer times and Christmas mornings, our basement the endless hours of rehearsal and our dining room countless great family meals. Even the bathroom has memories—mostly of crowding in there with my sisters, competing for mirror time while we were getting ready for church. However, it was one alone moment in that white-tiled room that completely changed my life.

When I was about eighteen, I was completely frustrated with my looks. For years I'd lived in the fishbowl of being a PK (pastor's kid), feeling like I never measured up to people's expectations of me. Every time I looked in the mirror, I told myself "My goodness, how fat. You look terrible today." It never seemed to get any better, and I felt worse and worse. A magazine story I read about a woman who had struggled with an eating disorder changed my life, but not the right way. Instead of being scared straight, I headed right down that road, developing my own eating disorder.

I amped up my workouts, going for two or three hours per day, and ate almost nothing. But it didn't work. I was not losing fast enough for me. So I tried even harder, eating even less and working out to the point of exhaustion. When I was nineteen, I found myself one day with my cheek pressed against the cold tile of the bathroom floor, with nothing left to give, no energy, no hope: I was done trying.

As I lay there, God touched my heart. He revealed to me that all my destructive efforts to shrink my body were not making me feel any better about myself. Instead, they made me feel worse, more insecure, emptier than ever. Although I'd been saved since I was a little kid, I still hadn't totally embraced God. It sounds funny, even bad to say this, but Jesus was "just" my savior, nothing more. I realized that I needed more than the promise of an eventual

heaven; I needed someone to walk through that pain with me right now. I needed someone to change my life, somebody to heal me.

At that moment, curled into a ball on that cold tile floor, I finally opened my heart to the Lord and completely gave my life, my flaws, my fears, everything, to Him. After hearing Bible verses and sermons for years, I finally heard Him speak to me. It wasn't a big booming voice like in the movies—but in my heart and mind I heard that still, small voice say He wanted to completely alter the way I view myself. I felt His sadness about how I'd been destroying the temple He'd created and realized that I'm truly beautiful in His eyes. He told me that He'd created me in His image for a specific time and purpose.

As I began to finally see just a glimpse of how God saw me, my heart literally broke and poured out the pain I'd been carrying for so long. But, as it drained of that sadness, He filled it up with love, acceptance and hope. I was so completely grateful for His healing that I pledged on that spot to love and serve Him for the rest of my life.

If someone ever buys our house, they'll make their own memories in its rooms. We'll still have our photo albums to remind us of the great times. But I'll always be able to remember the most amazing moment of all by simply looking into a mirror.

MIRROR

Mirror, Mirror on the wall, Have I got it?
'Cause Mirror you've always told me who I am
I'm finding it's not easy to be perfect
So sorry you won't define me
Sorry you don't own me

Who are you to tell me
That I'm less than what I should be?
Who are you? Who are you?
I don't need to listen

To the list of things I should do
I won't try, I won't try

Mirror I am seeing a new reflection
I'm looking into the eyes of He who made me
And to Him I have beauty beyond compare
I know He defines me

You don't define me, you don't define me

SUPERSTAR

Alyssa: You know those overly dramatic scenes in movies where the doctor sits the patient down, sets a manila folder of test results on the table between them and drops a huge bomb in that patient's life? That has happened to me.

Ever since I was little, I knew I wanted to be onstage; I wanted the bright lights, the applause, the flowers, the whole deal. I took dance classes, singing lessons, rehearsed in my room, did everything I could to prepare myself for what I considered my inevitable stardom on the Broadway stage. I reached the point where I was teaching voice & dance lessons, acting in one show, directing another. Rushing around one day, I fell down the stairs (my sister Lauren claims it was only one stair, but let's stick to the facts) and hurt my ankle badly. Really badly—the pain was unreal. After a day or two of ice and aspirin, the pain was only getting worse, so my mom took me to the doctor.

After a bunch of tests, the doctor sat me down just like in the movies and said I'd been diagnosed with RSD, a rare disease that usually hits senior citizens. I was freaking out inside as I listened to him describe Reflex Sympathetic Dystrophy, in which a patient's nerve endings start firing like crazy at the spot of an injury (in most patients, a broken hip), causing huge pain (that sounded way familiar to me). Eventually, he told me, all of my nerves would be firing like that, causing so much pain I'd end up in a wheelchair. He told us to come back the next day for the only treatment he knew of, clipping the big nerve that runs down the back of the leg, hopefully stopping the pain but leaving me with a "drop" foot. My choice was to do that and never dance again or skip it and end up unable to walk or function.

I was crushed. In an instant, everything I'd ever hoped for had been snatched away. As I limped to the car in tears, I remember my amazing mom saying, "We serve a healing God. How can that

surgery be in His plan?" We didn't go back the next day or the day after that. Instead, I spent the next two months pretty much trapped in my bedroom, torn up with incredible physical and spiritual pain. I was furious with God. I couldn't figure out how He could set a dream in my heart, give me the abilities to achieve it, then take it away in a heartbeat. I'm stubborn enough to hold out for an answer, so I kept praying. God responded with a simple question: "Lyssa, if you never did anything for Me again except lay in bed, how do you think I would feel about you?"

I realized I had a choice: I could turn my back on Him because He had stolen MY dream of stardom or I could humble myself. I didn't decide right away, but He began to soften my rock-hard heart. Eventually, He gave me the strength to pray "God, I'm okay if I never get a single word of praise from another person—the only thing I want is your love. It is the only thing that matters." That moment of brokenness was a huge turning point. As my heart softened over those weeks, the pain in my body began to go away. He healed my body as He healed my heart and, after a few months, I was pain free. It didn't matter that I might not sing another note or dance another step. Only after totally giving my life over to God's purpose did He begin to show me that HIS dream for my life looked a lot like the one I had chased with one difference: It would be for His glory, not mine. He would be the superstar, not me.

SUPERSTAR

Well I spent my life dreaming super dreams
But I hate to wake 'cause it's then I see
That I'm nothing more than a dreamer
Superstar in my dreams I'm a dreamer

See the lights of stardom were calling me
Because only then someone I would be
So my goal in life was to get there
Never satisfied

I wanna be a star
But is that all I'm really here for?
And if I'm not a star will that be okay?
Could I still be someone?
Guess I'm scared to wake from these super dreams
Scared to live the life that's been waiting for me
What would life be like with no bright lights?
Tell me who I'd be with no spotlight

God You'll have to say who I really am
'Cause I cannot live in this perfect dreamland
But I've heard Your dreams might be better
And I hope somehow

A superstar I may never be
And that is just a reality
Why can't we be God's superstars

CLOTHES

When you make a commitment not to date, you go on more than your share of sister date nights. A couple years ago, we all went to see a movie that was pretty popular at the time and were kinda shocked at the way the actresses in the movie were dressed. These were talented, young actresses with obvious smarts and great personalities who could carry a scene in their sleep. It just broke our hearts that, first, someone with authority on the movie set told these women to dress in those teeny, tiny clothes and, second, that these actresses had agreed to wear them. There on the big screen was living-color proof of how the world has degraded us as girls.

As we walked to the car, we talked about the lie we're told that we need to show our bodies to get attention. We got more and more irritated with the definition of beauty that requires people to be skinnier and skinnier so they can wear fewer, tighter clothes. Even though the movie was written as a comedy, we were thoroughly bummed by the time we got in the car. Becca passed on driving or shotgun so she could grab her guitar (How many times have we used that phrase? You must have a mental picture that she has one of those magic folding guitars that fits into her pocket. But she seriously has her guitar with her ALL THE TIME!) We started writing the song on the way home.

As we worked on the lyrics, we wanted to make sure it didn't sound like we were pointing the "frowning finger of judgment" in the face of girls who dress that way. Understanding the pressure we all feel to conform, we wanted to take a quirky approach and let people know that we understand. Everyone needs a reminder to focus on chasing God, to find out how He sees us, to learn what about us matters to Him. As much as we wanted girls to see the craziness of chasing the world's approval (that never lasts) by dressing worse every time, we also wanted guys to understand we

need their help. How great would it be if guys would encourage girls who dress modestly? Girls may not know this, but there are tons of guys who are trying to keep their hearts and minds pure as well, guys who would benefit from seeing fewer square feet of exposed skin every day. We just hope this song gives guys and girls both the courage to not just sort of accept modesty, but to be proud of it and wear their clothes that actually fit them as a sign of who they really are in Christ. And, we hope they'll remember that the clothes they wear are secondary to how they dress on the inside, with a character that truly honors God.

CLOTHES

Clothes aren't what they used to be
They don't seem to fit you and me anymore
Modesty is out the door
Flaunting what we've got and more is in
Yeah it's in

They're saying
Don't ask why just wear what we say
You'll look like a model if you'll only obey
To get the attention, just do what we say

Pay so much for clothes so small
Was this shirt made for me or my doll?
Is this all I get?
I looked so hot but caught a cold
I was doing just what I was told
To fit in

We're saying let's ask why
Don't wear what they say
Don't want to be a model
They can't eat anyway
That kind of attention will fade with the day
So I'll stand up and say

Clothes that fit are fine
Won't show what's mine
Don't change my mind
I'll be fine

SHE WALKED AWAY

Do you know anyone who lives with one foot out the door? People who are always dissatisfied with their life, talking about and waiting for the next better thing? When we were younger, we met a girl who took that approach. She happened to be our neighbor over the back fence and a lot of fun to be with. We quickly became friends. She was adventuresome and funny with a unique perspective on life. But, she also had that faraway look in her eye and pushed back on her parents on a lot of issues. One day, we got word that our friend had run away. Apparently, one of her episodes of pushing back had escalated into an argument and she'd left, apparently for good.

That hit us really hard. We had seen TV shows about runaways and commercials for runaway hotlines, but we'd never known anyone who had just taken off like that. It really bothered us to think of our friend hiding somewhere alone, angry and scared. When we heard her parents talk about how much they missed her, saw their tear-streaked faces as they discussed the incredible pain in their hearts, it floored us. We'd read the parable of the Prodigal Son a million times, but we'd never really understood the pain a parent feels when a child runs off until that moment. That realization also gave us this fleeting glimpse of how God must feel when His own children (i.e. us, you, and everyone else) take off on Him and seek out their own version of living.

As we trip through life, we all get so convinced that we have the right answers, that we often turn our backs on our heavenly daddy and His amazing love, guidance and protection. But we know from scripture how overjoyed the father was to welcome home his son, and that we get the same joyful, loving reception from God when we turn back to Him. That story inspires us to keep turning back to Him, to keep moving closer, to set aside our ideas of how life would be if only we were completely in charge of our destiny

and finally surrender and fall into His arms. It is that story of our long-lost friend, who was lost in her heart as much as she was gone from her home, viewed through the lens of scripture, that drove us to write this song. Those two stories, both incredibly real, remind us to stop living with one foot out the door of God's house.

SHE WALKED AWAY

She couldn't take one more day
Home was more her prison now
Independence called out
She had to get it

A fight was all she needed
To give her reason
She slammed the door with no goodbye
And knew that it was time

Now she's driving too fast
She didn't care to glance behind
And through her tears she laughed
It's time to kiss the past goodbye

I'm finally on my own
Don't try to tell me no
There's so much more for me
Just watch what I will be

She walked away
Couldn't say why she was leaving
She walked away
She left all she had believed in
She walked away

Not a day goes by
For the ones she's left behind
They're always asking why
And thoughts of her consume their mind

God please let her know
The love we tried to show
We'd promise anything
If you'd just bring her home

Tell her we love her
Tell her she's wanted
One more thing God
Tell her please come home
Please come home

The choice is yours alone now
Tell me how this story ends

AVERAGE GIRL

Like we assume most girls in America do, we grew up re-e-e-ally looking forward to our sixteenth birthday. Sure, the driver's license thing would be cool, but, most of all, we were excited about reaching the age limit our parents had set for us to start dating. The big 1-6 was the milestone of milestones, the big day we'd always looked forward to, where we could live the dream portrayed in so many movies, books, and conversations. In our usual optimistic way, we kind of just assumed that we'd magically have a boyfriend on that day—most likely we'd open up a big box at our birthday party and, "boom," out would walk Mr. Right. So, we were all counting down the days when God started to change our minds.

It began when He convicted our Mom and Dad to examine their own dating life, to discover what good it had brought into their marriage. They asked God to show them how dating had helped or hurt them personally, how it affected their relationship today, and what they could or should have done differently? What He showed them wasn't very positive. So, one day, they sat us down for a family meeting and shared this question that God had placed on their hearts, "Is dating really part of God's plan for us?" They didn't grab a bullhorn and order us not to date. Instead, they lovingly challenged us to pursue His answer as a family.

At first we were terrified and a little annoyed: How dare they threaten our dream of true love? But, we agreed to seek God's direction through prayer, reading, and listening to tapes—partly because we hoped that dating would be part of God's calling on our lives. As we worked our way through that process, we discovered that God wanted our single years for His purposes. It turns out that He wasn't robbing us of an important experience, but hoping to protect our hearts. After hours of "Are you sure?" prayers, we decided to trust Him and wait on His timing for us. We agreed not to date. It was tough, and a little scary, to let go of

our dreams of teen romance, but obeying Him and trusting Him for the ultimate reward was worth it.

Now, if you think that everyone around us gave our decision a standing ovation, you'd be wrong. We took a lot of grief from people who said that approach was weird, totally Stone Age, just not normal. Someone even made fun of us, saying, "So, what, you're like Sleeping Beauty and some day you're just going to wake up and your Prince Charming will ride up on a horse?" When our Mom heard that, she told us to think of God's approach at the very beginning—"He made one Adam and one Eve, not five Eves so Adam could date his way through them until he found the right one." Instead, He basically told Adam: "Rest in me. When you wake up, I'll have what you need." He was pretty much the original Sleeping Beauty.

With encouragement like that, we stayed committed to our decision. It hasn't always been easy—we'd see cute guys and think "Couldn't we have just one date?" But as we stuck together, prayed together, structured our social life around outings with groups of like-minded people, and devoted our energies to serving God, His peace really began to take hold in our hearts. As we stayed His course, He gave us the strength and confidence to not only keep our commitment but to stand up and speak our mind. That's where the tone of this song comes from: It's a lovingly defiant declaration of our values and vision as women of God. (It also makes it clear that we don't hate boys—we think it's a very pro-boy song.) But, overall, it's an expression of a hugely important part of our life, offered as an encouragement to girls and guys to set aside the world's approach, to stop dating other people's future spouses and instead, focus on Him and His purposes for their lives. There is nothing at all average about that.

AVERAGE GIRL

So what I'm not your average girl
I don't meet the standards of this world
Chasing after boys is not my thing
See I'm waiting for a wedding ring
No more dating
I'm just waiting
Like Sleeping Beauty
My prince will come for me
No more dating
I'm just waiting
'Cause God is writing my love story
Boys are bad that's certainly not true
'Cause God's preparing one for you
If you get tired waiting till he comes
God's arms are the perfect place to run

Sleep that's the only thing
For me 'cause when I sleep God's
Preparing one for me

SURRENDER

Alyssa: People talk about dreams and visions all the time, but do you really know the difference? In the dictionary, both words have pretty long definitions. Outside of the kind you have when you go to sleep after eating spicy food, a dream is defined as an ambition (which, in turn, is described as an eager or strong desire to achieve a desirable goal.) I had all kinds of dreams growing up—I saw myself on the stage of a Broadway theater, singing and dancing my way into the hearts of the audience.

As you might know from having read the chapter about our song, "Superstar," I was pretty much wiped out by my struggle with RSD (reflex sympathetic dystrophy) when I was 18. The body that God had given me to dance with didn't work right any more. I was in so much pain I didn't want to talk much less sing. I withdrew from my dream-related activities and spent some time being pretty angry. But, all the while, I was asking God questions. "Why me?" was a favorite as was "When will this end?" As I look back over my journals from that time, I see myself struggling big-time with Him for control of my life. I asked God straight up, "What is going to happen to my life if I open my hands to You?" I basically confessed that I didn't trust Him enough to let go, to take my hands off the steering wheel of my life.

After months of struggling physically and wrestling spiritually, His persistent love finally wore down my resistance. Amazingly, as my own personal dreams and ambitions leaked away, God filled up the hole it left with an amazing vision. Now there's a key difference there. The dictionary describes vision as the experience of seeing as if with the eyes of God. My dreams were my creation, my version of the future I had chosen. God's vision was entirely different—it was His revelation of His plan, His explanation of why He made me the way He did. He began to show me, my sisters and my parents His purpose for us. He wanted to use our talents His way for His

purposes, for us to carry His message of hope to an abandoned generation wandering in a lost world. And this vision would only come about if each of us, me included, would surrender to Him every day.

SURRENDER

My hands hold safely to my dreams
Clutching tightly not one has fallen
So many years I've shaped each one
Reflecting my heart showing who I am
Now You're asking me to show
What I'm holding oh so tightly
Can't open my hands can't let go
Does it matter?
Should I show You?
Can't You let me go?

Surrender, Surrender You whisper gently
You say I will be free
I know but can't You see?
My dreams are me, My dreams are me

You say You have a plan for me
And that You want the best for my life
Told me the world had yet to see
What You can do with one
That's committed to Your calling
I know of course what I should do
That I can't hold these dreams forever
If I give them now to You
Will You take them away forever?
Or can I dream again?

Becca gives Otto a guitar lesson during the recording of "Another Journal Entry"

Lyssa proves there's no such thing as a bad hair day in the studio.

Anyone would look like a rock star in this light.

Next time we'll choose a studio that's not built on the side of a hill.

The 2006 Dove Awards were great; our friends Beka and Audrey made it the best.

We never had little brothers 'til we met the guys in Stellar Kart.

Becca has the longest arms so she takes our party pics everywhere we go.

We were kidding when we put the eight-foot-tall ice cream cone in our rider...

Our cousin, Sarah Barlow, is a crazy cool photographer. (We mention that because she took this amazing picture.)

Lauren & Zac from Day of Fire compare the drummer badges of honor: big callouses.

When Lifeway shoots a video, even an old tunnel makes a good setting.

Can you believe this is our friend's backyard?

Living on camera: part of the deal.

This is how we pack for a quick overnighter...

Liz, our makeup artist, autographs Becca's face.

Lauren battles the brain freeze from the giant ice cream cone..

Europe will never be the same after we rocked with the Day of Fire guys.

...and your little dog too.

Our first day in our new home (on wheels). Life on the tour bus begins...

The Fender company lent us a pile of sweet gear for this photo shoot—maybe someday we'll learn to play them...

So bummed Prince Charming doesn't really live here. Trust us, we checked.

We're glad Lauren can sleep anywhere, but behind the wheel isn't the greatest idea ...

"So, gray hair is a sign of dignity, right?"

Lauren envies our mad jumping skeelz.

Can you guess which BarlowGirl is hiding behind those shades?

Lauren gets her minimum daily requirement of rock.

The kick-jump lessons from Kutless pay off big time.

Wrapping up the tour with Kutless & Stellar Kart.

The most important part of show prep: quiet time.

Some bands use treadmills to stay in shape, but we're not "some bands."

Becca who?

Becca tries to convince us that harmonizing is singing too...

How to draw a big crowd: open for Switchfoot.

Rockin' the morning news in Nashville and all anyone wants to see is the weather report.

Grey may be your favorite color, but I won't give up my sequins.

"So, I guess we're out of road."

"I can't believe they think we're actually playing."

Lyssa rocks a microphone older than her for the "Grey" video.

The Rebecca St. James tour team photo.

Becca unplugged.

Even our food ends up on camera.

We love SHINE FM, our hometown station in Chicago. And they love us right back.

And, for the finale, hamsters jump through Lauren's giant hoops.

The legendary end-of-tour bus party. And, yes, a pinata gave its life for our enjoyment.

I'm sure happy I wrote the chords on my wrist. Now if I could only see the lyrics on my bicep.

Becca rocks the kind folks at Napster.

Where else would we celebrate Lauren's 20th birthday but at an aquarium.

BarlowGirl: The Life

(STORIES FROM THE ROAD)

Once our first album was born, our lives kept changing really, really fast. It seemed like, one day, we were doing our everyday thing: Becca was teaching art classes, Alyssa was doing local plays, Lauren was finishing up her home school routine. Then BOOM (that's a big boom, like sonic boom big), we're in a different town every day, meeting new people, learning how to keep it together onstage when everything goes wrong. Our parents realized early on that, if we didn't get a routine together, we would fall apart. So, this section offers a little peek at life on the road, based on our typical daily schedule. Oh, and since our days get a little weird with traveling, performing and all that, we'll start at the stroke of midnight.

MIDNIGHT – ON THE ROAD

When a new day actually starts, we're usually on our tour bus, trying to wind down as we roar down the road to the next city on our tour. Our hair is usually wet from having showered after our show and we're in jammies (Alyssa likes the ones with the feet on them—just kidding.) Our favorite way to unwind is to watch a movie of some kind. We love musicals—we've probably seen Oklahoma, Funny Girl, and My Fair Lady a hundred times each—and comedies. You'd think that, after performing most of the day that we'd be tired of music, but that kind of stuff really relaxes us and recharges our batteries. After a while, the "bus noise," the roar of the engine and the ever present hum of the AC, combines with the gentle sway of a moving bus and our own fatigue and it's off to sleep.

Gotta tell you, we lo-o-o-o-ve our bus. Back when we were getting in the whole music thing, we would drive to our shows in Dad's car with all of our gear crammed into the trunk or our laps. Little by little, things got bigger and better for us. When we started touring after the release of our first CD, we tried traveling in a van, but, with five people, instruments and several boxes of t-shirts, that got really crowded really quickly. We added a trailer to carry our gear, but we still flirted with claustrophobia every time we hit the road. So, we looked around at our options and upgraded to one of those camper deals. That was fun, but the routine of driving for hours then setting up our stuff then packing it up and driving to the next town was turning our dad into a zombie. Something had to change.

We started looking around for a tour bus and actually found one online. It was owned by a famous country music star who had fixed it up to be a haven for her and her family on the road, so it was just right for us. Nowadays, we each get our own bunk with curtains so we can sleep peacefully even if someone else is still

awake. It has a sweet kitchen so our mom can bake us stuff when we're kinda homesick and a dining area we can use to study, eat or play cards.

We still feel most at home in our house near Chicago, but the bus is a huge part of our ability to tour well. Like everything else in our life, God waited until we were thankful for something before he'd give us the next thing.

6:39 A.M. – ON THE AIR

Why do radio stations schedule their morning shows in the actual morning? Couldn't we just sleep for five more minutes? Why do we have to brush our hair for a radio interview? These are just a few of the questions three cranky sisters have been known to ask when the alarm goes off in the morning. We love radio people, but how on earth are they so cheerful so early in the morning? However, since radio interviews are a huge part of letting people know where we'll be playing, we start a lot of days with an interview either in studio or over the phone. Phone is better—the tooth brush can wait. Then it's back on the bus and, hopefully, back to sleep.

We remember one radio station in particular. We had stopped by the California studios of Air 1 Radio during their pledge drive. While we were on the air, they took a call from a listener who shared an amazing story from his life. Working as a tow truck driver, he had recently stopped on the side of the road to help a lady whose car had died. Like he always did on calls, he kept his truck doors open and his radio playing so he could listen to some uplifting music while he worked. As he hitched up this lady's car, our song, Never Alone, came on the air. As he connected cables and checked brakes, he noticed that his customer was not only listening, but crying as well.

Not sure how to react, he gently approached her and asked if everything was okay. She answered that things had been really tough for her lately. Then, through her tears, she asked what the song was about, specifically, who it was about, and how someone could reach the point of never feeling alone. Over the next 45 minutes, he took roadside assistance to a whole new level as he explained God's love for her and His offer of eternal life. Before they parted company, she prayed to accept Jesus into her life and went on her way.

When we heard that story, we were blown away. God is so

amazing—only He could use a little song that came out of a terrible time in our life to reach a woman with a broken-down life sitting in a broken-down car. That radio station visit left us soaring, ready to do more for God.

9:07 A.M. – IN A NEW TOWN

When you start your snoozin' to the rumble of a bus engine, your eyes pop wide open when it stops. It's weird to go to bed in one town or state and wake up in a totally different place, but it's exciting, too. We all look forward to getting our first peek at a new town, to see what's shakin'. Sometimes we look out the window and see mountains (usually when we're in a state with mountains) and other times it's the desert or just a big brick wall. Such is the joy of life on the road. First priority? Coffee.

No matter how far we travel, we could never outrun the Internet (not that we'd want to, of course.). Because of the community that has developed through our website, we have relationships in nearly every town we visit. We launched a basic version of BarlowGirl. com sometime in 2003 when we were just getting rolling, but knew it could do a lot more than just present our information. We really wanted to get a message board going because we sensed that our fans would really enjoy it. We sing about such emotional issues that we wanted our listeners to have an outlet for their thoughts and a community to find support in their personal struggles. The SoundPost message board section went live right around the time our first CD was released and the response was instantaneous and overwhelming. We read it all the time and post our own thoughts as well. We want our fans to know what we believe and that we genuinely care about them.

Over the past two years, more than 4,500 users from all over the world have registered and posted more than half a million messages (total, not each.) Our brother, Josh, and his wife, Sabrina, run our site and, although they're tech geniuses, even they couldn't monitor that much board traffic. So, we started recruiting moderators (we call them "mods") from among our friends, heavy board users and our most committed fans. They are more than syntax police: they are an amazing group of spiritually

mature people who have become our friends and the leaders of some amazing online support groups.

In a lot of ways, the mods are like online pastors; they answer the kids' spiritual questions, they moderate conflict, they encourage posters to get help with really serious issues. We have posters who struggle with eating disorders, cutting, suicidal urges, scary stuff. Depression is a big problem as well—there's peer pressure, school stress, strife at home, parental divorce—so we're glad to help in some way. Although we post as often as we can, the real ministry happens when the groups really rally to each other's needs. Time and time again, these kids find encouragement, biblical truth and hope in this amazing online community.

Our relationship with the online community isn't completely electronic, though. It seems like any time we pass within a couple hundred miles of an active board participant, they make it to our shows, no matter what. When they get together, the energy goes through the roof, both in their reunions and during our shows. It's cool to see that they're often more psyched to see each other than our performance. The relationships we've developed with these amazing people and the ministry they do together is a blessing beyond anything we could have imagined when we launched our site. We thank God for them and the fact that, because of our online community, we're never strangers in any town we visit.

1:14 P.M. – JOURNAL TIME

Time to write the latest entry in our tour journal. Lauren has become the de facto chronicler of all things BarlowGirl, with occasional inputs from Alyssa. It pretty much takes an act of Congress to get Becca to post a journal entry, but she's a very active poster on the SoundPost section of our website. The beauty of wireless web allows us to post stuff from pretty much anywhere, so we talk, we write, we post and continue our day.

Some people think we let people know too much about ourselves, particularly on our website. They tell us to be careful because "there's a lotta kooks out there." That is definitely true. We live in a fallen world and sin is a factor in every life. But we believe that God wants us to share what's going on in our lives to help people realize they're not alone in their struggles. If we talk honestly about what we're dealing with, at least two good things can happen. One, our transparency will challenge people to accept us as we are instead of elevating us onto some pedestal. Secondly, we hope our honesty can encourage them to employ the same clarity in their communications with family and friends. It's not easy to tell someone when a sin has you by the heel, but that confession is the first step toward forgiveness and letting God into the middle of a struggle.

Some of the stories that have surfaced on our message board have been amazing. We've heard from one poster who was literally standing in her bedroom with a knife in her hand, on the verge of taking her life, when one of our songs came on and stopped her in her tracks. Another poster from Australia wrote about giving a copy of our first CD to a friend who was in secular group therapy for an eating disorder. This friend ended up sharing our music with her group and they now listen to it as part of their approach to healing. We hear story after story of God using our music to give kids the courage to tell someone and seek help for their

struggles with cutting, pornography, addiction, and countless other challenges. Maybe it's just us, but we can't imagine that these kinds of conversations are happening every day in the school hallway, in the lunch room, wherever. Our online community offers just enough anonymity that posters can get comfortable sharing what needs to get fixed in their lives. Any good that happens is God's deal, but we'll keep the flow of communication going so He can continue using us in His efforts to change lives.

2:30 P.M. – SOUNDCHECK

We play our concerts in just about every kind of building you could imagine. We do a lot of churches, but we've also played in stadiums, civic centers, even a cruise ship one time. Once the afternoon gets rolling, it's time for soundcheck. And, believe us, every building, every sound system is different. We carry just about all of our own gear, but every room has a different shape with different echoes, different tones. So, we gotta soundcheck. We plug in, tune up, and run through as many songs as it takes before we think we sound right and our sound guy gives us the thumbs-up. Soundcheck can also be a chance to try out a new song or just crank out an old favorite. Then we gotta bail so the other artists we're with can soundcheck too.

Since we got rolling with this music thing, we have been blessed with the chance to tour and/or play with some amazing artists. One of the first to show serious faith in us was Todd Agnew. We first met him during a show we played in the fall of 2003 before our CD came out. He invited us to dinner, so we all headed out to a local burger place after the concert. (When you're a musician on the road, you eat a lot of late dinners. So you're limited to places that are still serving food at midnight. It can be quite an experience.) Over dinner, he mentioned it would be great to tour together someday. Just a few months later, we got a call from our booking agent who said the tour invitation was for real. It sounded great to us. We were still pretty unknown and, quite frankly, he wasn't.

As the tour got rolling, we discovered that Todd's abilities as a musician, songwriter and singer actually take a backseat to his passion for developing other artists. On the typical tour, the headliner usually gets the best of the best—the best times for performance and soundchecks, the best location for their merchandise table, the entire spotlight at show's end, all that—

because they've earned it. Todd took the totally opposite track with us.

He continually told his audiences to support the other bands on the bill, gave us the best spot in the lobby for our merch table, and even invited us and the other band to join him onstage for the finale of his set a couple of times. In doing so, he helped us grow in our confidence and build more awareness of our music across the country. He didn't have to do that, but he is just one of those guys who is at peace with how God made him and just radiates that comfort and confidence into other people.

Since that tour, we've had the chance to tour with other amazing people like tobyMac and Rebecca St. James and shared the stage with amazing artists like Mac Powell of Third Day and David Crowder. We've practically developed a whole 'nother family composed of the bands we've toured with. You spend that kind of time together, you either want to kill each other or become family. To date, God has kept us happily in the peaceful family category.

4:46 P.M. – GET DRESSED

Time to get ready. Maybe some day we'll work out a way to take turns doing the clothes-hair-makeup thing, but old habits die hard. Ever since we were little, we've always piled into the bathroom together to get ready, asking each other's opinion on an outfit, elbowing each other in front of the mirror. We are sisters, after all. Some people who have seen us play and/or met us for the first time have asked us how we can sing songs like "Mirror" and "Clothes" then go onstage in clothes that we looked at in a mirror. Well, that's a great question. Our short answer is that beauty is something that God designed into women—the world has just gotten it all messed up.

Maybe the most memorable "getting ready" experience happened not long after we'd signed with Fervent Records. We'd heard that Susan Riley, the label's founder and president, was going to be at the show, but were still surprised when she showed up two hours early. We were even more surprised when she said, "What can I do to help?" then grabbed an iron. It would be one thing if we hadn't signed on yet and she was trying to persuade us to come aboard, but it was another thing entirely to have the woman who runs the company we now worked for ironing our show clothes and helping carry our gear.

From the first time we had lunch with her, we knew she was way different from a lot of industry types we'd met. As we've gotten to know her, we have discovered a woman who is truly committed to doing things her way, the right way. She runs her label like a family, trying to make business decisions based on a mix of scripture, common sense and what's best for the people involved. One example of that is the way she treated us AFTER we signed. She was anxious to get us into the studio to start recording BarlowGirl, so we agreed to a pretty fast timeline. To make us feel more comfortable while we were in the studio, she and her husband moved out of their

home and let us move in for three months. Go back and read that last sentence again: The head of one of the hottest labels in the Christian music industry cleared out of her own house so we could feel at home while recording. That's just not done, but that's how she rolls.

She has told us more than once that we are an answer to years of prayers. (What a coincidence—she's an answer to our prayers as well.) Since they founded the label, she and her husband had been asking God to provide a girl band for their artist lineup at Fervent. Having found great comfort in music as a young girl, part of her dream for the company was to use music to speak hope into the lives of girls. She was just looking for the right girl band to do that. Throughout our relationship, she has supported and encouraged us at every turn. If you've ever had the chance to work with a leader who is confident enough in herself and her faith to serve the people in her organization, you know it is an amazing gift. By serving us, she has helped us get ready to do our best onstage and off.

6:00 P.M. – FAMILY DEVOTIONS

With the daily grind of life, the demands on our time, the decisions we have to make as a family, we'd probably go crazy without our daily family devotionals. Otherwise known as "devo," this is a time for us to open our Bibles, share from our journals and pray about what's buggin' us at the moment. Spending time in His word gives our family a chance to remember that He is the source of every good thing. We use that time to ask His guidance on His vision for us, our family, our music and our ministry. These sweet times have been a part of our life as far back as we can remember, thanks to our parents. We appreciate them more than you'll ever know.

There are people in the music business who have told us that keeping our parents around is a huge mistake. To be honest, the track record of our type of arrangement is not strong—the winding path of music history is littered with the smoking ruins of families that have tried to work together and failed. We are trusting God that He will defend our approach since it was His idea in the first place. After our relationship with God, our family relationship is the most important thing in our lives.

If you've been reading this book in order, you know that our dad was the first performer in our little family. He grew up writing and performing his own songs and encountered a nice degree of success, touring the country and sharing his art with tons of people. A lot of dads with four kids would have looked forward to time on the road as a welcome break, but our dad was different. He hated being away from his family, so he brought us along as his band. Then, after a prompting from God, he called a family meeting one day and told us he was stepping aside from his performing career so that he could manage us.

Although he was a total stranger to the intricacies of "the business," he has worked like a mule to learn which way the wheels

turn and how decisions are wisely made. The way we see it, there is no way that a random manager working for just a paycheck would defend us and our best interests the way he does. He bravely serves as our voice to the industry, representing us with integrity, honesty and strength. If nothing else, his ability to survive as the only male on a tour bus with four women is proof of his strength and God's protection.

When it comes to fierce defenders, only our Mom can hold a candle to Dad. She is the most amazing woman we've ever met anywhere. Once, when she was home-schooling us, she devoted a season to studying the woman portrayed in Proverbs 31. At first, we wondered why the printed words seemed so familiar to us, but then we realized we'd been watching her live out those words every day. She applies her great business sense to our merchandise sales and creates a home for us on the road. She constantly brings touches of home onto our tour bus like fresh-baked cookies after a concert or completely decorating the place for the major holidays.

As great as she does with the material things, her greatest strength is intercessory prayer. She is a bonafide prayer warrior, constantly encouraging us while pressing into God to claim His promises for our family. From her, we're continually learning what it means to be a woman, a wife, a mother and a friend who is fiercely committed to God. She's the one who sees it when our attitudes start to slip and reminds us what it means to worship God as a lifestyle.

Even now, we run into people who ask "You're in your twenties, why do you still need your mommy and daddy to prop you up?" Our answer to them is simple: They're more than parents to us. In our personal, artistic and professional relationships, they're mentors who provide accountability on our personal integrity and maintain a safe environment for us. In their devotion to God and their family, they clear a path for us so we can focus on the ministry and music God has given to us. Because of their devotion to our family, we have the strength to do what God has called us to do.

7:35 P.M. – TIME TO PLAY

No matter how many times we do it, we still get a huge kick out of playing and singing our music for people. Our audience can be two friends sitting on our tour bus or thousands of people in a stadium, but our outlook is the same: We want to bless you. We pray a lot about our motivation and check our hearts constantly to make sure we are headed onstage for the right reason. God gave us our talent, our songs and our opportunities as a way to direct people's attention His way, to glorify Him. If it ever becomes anything else, we owe it to Him, ourselves and everyone else to switch off our amps and go home for good.

It's amazing nowadays to see how comfortable Becca is onstage. When we get rolling, she's a regular maniac, jumping around, swinging her arm on power chords, talking directly to the audience. Trust us, she hasn't always been that way. When we were kids, she avoided the limelight like the plague. While Alyssa was singing onstage in the children's ministry at our church, Becca always preferred to work in the nursery, holding babies and staying out of sight. Although she was learning guitar, she played it mostly for herself. One day, our dad mentioned that his bass player was not available for an upcoming weekend and invited her to fill in. Oddly enough, she did.

We still remember the first time she took the stage at children's church—she stood all the way to the back, trying to blend into the scenery. She would have stood in another room if she could have. When the first song kicked off, she remained perfectly still, staring at her feet as she played. She did the entire worship set (and many, many more after that) looking more like a statue than a bass player. She sounded great, but looked like she wanted to disappear.

As time went on, Becca switched to guitar and we transitioned from our dad's backup band to our own group. Still, her onstage

approach didn't change. Alyssa would jump around like she'd stuck her finger in a socket, Lauren's arms would be flailing like she was directing a speeding airplane to park and Becca would be perfectly still. Out of frustration, Lauren took to tossing things at her while we played, thinking a flinch would be better than no movement at all. After months of no motion, we took the drastic step of putting a big mirror on the wall of our rehearsal room so she could see what she looked like. With that visual feedback and Lauren's constant urging, Becca started to move around a little bit more with every song. But, the minute we'd step in front of a live audience, she'd turn back to stone.

Becca understood the impact her shyness was having, so she started taking it to God every day in her prayer time. Before long, He revealed to her that she was paralyzed by the fear of what people think. As she studied, God brought some encouraging verses to her attention, so she started writing them on sticky notes and posting them all over the place. When we'd set up to play, she'd open up her Bible to a favorite verse and lay it on her foot pedal board as a reminder. She even started writing the verses on her wrist so that, when she was playing, she could look down and see them up close.

It took a couple months of study, prayer and practice, but God was renewing her mind. She realized that there were worse things in the world than tiny musical errors and playing louder was the best way to enjoy performing. One day, in a show we were doing right after we signed with Fervent, it was like someone plugged in the Becca doll and she started moving around. We were so stoked, we almost stopped playing. When we wrapped up and came off stage, our dad hugged her and told her she did great. Considering just how painfully shy she'd always been, we knew that we had all witnessed a miracle.

9:27 P.M. – SIGNING TABLE
(OR ATTACK OF THE FLYING SHARPIES)

At the conclusion of the entire show, we troop over to a table where we get a chance to go one-on-one with our listeners. It still feels a little odd to be the center of attention, but we meet so many amazing people at those tables that we've come to love it. People bring us remarkable hand-made gifts that reflect the impact our music has had on their life, others pose for photos or share stories of what our music has meant to them. We sign clothes, ticket stubs, grocery receipts, pretty much anything people can grab and put under our flying Sharpies. Those interactions at the autograph tables are a daily reminder of why we do what we do—it's because God loves His people and wants us to tell them that.

Signing autographs may be the absolute weirdest part of doing what God has called us to do. All along the way, we've pretty much focused on the music and the way God was using it to heal issues, both in our lives and other people's. The stuff that comes along with performing, like autographs, didn't really cross our mind until people started asking for them. Scratching our name on something that wasn't a birthday card made us uncomfortable, so we tried to avoid it. The first time someone asked Becca for her autograph, she looked at the person with a stunned look and simply asked, "Why?" None of us was that excited about signing stuff because we had started the whole music thing to glorify God, not ourselves. To us, it seemed like signing autographs would have the opposite effect. But, after each show we did, more and more people approached us for our autographs, freaking us out more each time. We needed some help.

We prayed hard about the issue. We hated turning people away, but we really didn't like the nagging sense that each signature pushed us a little farther up the stairs of a pedestal. God responded gently with a different perspective. He reminded us that, yes, the

music was about Him, not us, and that He was using it to mend the broken and find the lost. We also started to realize that, as the pace of our life and the frenzy of our appearances picked up steam, our time at the signing table was about our only chance to interact one-on-one with the people God was touching. His fresh perspective on autographs changed everything.

Since then, we have completely fallen in love with our time at the signing table. Even if we have a terrible show full of mistakes, we get an instant boost from some of the most encouraging people on the planet. As we sit there, our Sharpies swirling across CDs, shirts, sneakers, ticket stubs, paper cups, whatever people can find, we hear stories of how God has worked in people's lives through our music, of friendships established on our message board, of families who are attending their first concert together, one amazing thing after another. (We also receive the most amazing handmade gifts from people, from curio boxes plastered with our pictures to miniature replicas of us onstage. We should probably start a Signing Line Museum someday.)

We consider our time at the signing table a blessing, a genuine gift from God. Whether we're tired from a long week or hopped up from a great show, we take time to pray before each sitting to ensure we're ready to make the most of each of those mini-conversations. Knowing God can change lives with a single word, we choose ours in hopes He'll use them to heal one person, inspire another or open a door in someone's life for Him to walk through. Opportunities like that make it hard to wait for our next autograph session.

BACK ON THE BUS

By the time we finish up our post-concert signing line, it's usually close to 11pm. After running around like madwomen for most of the typical concert day, missing meals for appointments and performing under hot lights, we are usually a lovely combination of sweaty, tired and hungry. (If we could each nap while eating dinner in the shower, we would, but most food doesn't mix well with running water.) Fortunately, our standard performance contract includes a couple of hotel rooms, so, while the road crew is breaking down the stage, we leave the concert venue behind and zip over to our rooms for a quick bunch of showers. Then, after we get cleaned up, the tour caravan arrives at the hotel and it's on to the next town.

That time between cleaning up and hitting the road is when the most fun usually happens on tour. The day's work is done and no one is really thinking about tomorrow's show, so people tend to be more relaxed and cheerful. Of all the good times we had on the Rebecca St. James tour in the spring of 2006, there was probably none better than the now-legendary BarlowGirl Dance Party and Omelet Cook Off.

We had just wrapped up the first leg of the 40-show tour and the crews were starting to settle into a routine. That process takes longer on some tours than others, but it went quickly this time because the people Rebecca surrounds herself with are absolutely phenomenal. Not only were her musicians incredibly talented and their crew really skilled, but they were also good guys, the kind of people you feel safe around because they just might love Jesus more than you do.

In that environment, we were able to let down our guard a little bit and even invite some of their team onto our bus. (The list of people we normally allow on our bus is re-e-e-e-ally short. Even though it has wheels, it's our home, so we don't use it for interviews

or business meetings or meet & greets. There are better places for that stuff.) After wrapping up our post-show routine, it seemed like everyone had the same idea—find some food. We all ended up at the backstage catering area, disappointed because there was nothing there but some stale donuts from breakfast. The guys got even more bummed when Alyssa said "Oh well, guess I'll go back to our bus and make something in our kitchen." Since all they had on their bus was a microwave, coated on the inside with exploded burrito, they were a little jealous. So, Lauren, ever a sucker for the puppy-dog face, invited them all onto our bus.

The living room area of our bus can fit eight people comfortably, so it was a little cozy with fifteen people wedged in there. The vibe was great, though. One guy brought his stash of bagels and Rebecca St. James took over the stove, cooking her signature omelets for everyone. As the hostesses, it was our job to provide music, so we plugged an iPod into the sound system. We were about two songs into our rock playlist when inspiration struck: It was 80's music time! We dug into our stash and pulled out our six-disc set of 80's hits and lit the fuse of a great party.

Inspired by our musical choice, Rebecca revealed a tradition from her ancestral homeland. It turns out that Australians have a thing called a "bush dance." It's kind of like a hoedown featuring choreographed dances, food and fun. When the group yelled for an example, Rebecca and her brother, Joel, agreed to spring their dance on us. Off they went down the center aisle, narrowly missing people's toes, showing us how to dance, Aussie-style. When they reached the front of the bus, Beka Hardt, our dear friend and full-time helper, stood up, hushed the crowd and said she could top that. In her uniquely hilarious style, she worked her way down the aisle with a classic routine. Like so often happens in these volatile situations, a dance-off had erupted without warning. One after another, people took their turn in the aisle, struttin' their signature moves.

In that instant, we were transformed from professional peers seeking respect in a tough industry into a bunch of twenty-something dorks demonstrating their lamest high school dance moves. It was an absolutely great time and a wonderful bonding experience for the tour. Experiences like that, where people can be themselves and relationships are strengthened, are not limited to the music world or a tour bus. It's the sort of thing that can happen anywhere. Because, the indisputable truth is that we're all just regular people, trying to worship God with our lives and build some positive relationships along the way.

BarlowGirl: The Followup

(BEHIND THE SONGS ON *ANOTHER JOURNAL ENTRY*)

People say you have your whole life to write your first album and about twelve months for your second one. That's pretty close to true. After our first CD, BarlowGirl, *hit stores in February 2004, we launched into a whirlwind schedule of promotion and touring in the U.S. and overseas. As you might have guessed from reading the previous section, life on the road doesn't allow for a lot of down time, a critical element in the creative process. We managed to write a few songs on the road, but we were still a little short on usable tunes. By the time November 2004 rolled around, it was crunch time. So, we celebrated Christmas by shutting off the phones, getting out our journals and heading back to the living room. Thankfully, our Christmas gift from God that year was enough songs to fill our next album,* Another Journal Entry.

GREY

Y ou might not ever admit this to anyone, but have you ever felt like you'd give almost anything to be popular? In those times when you're alone, when you see other people getting all the attention, when you see that one little crowd of people laughing about some joke you'll never hear, do you ever think acceptance might be worth any sacrifice? That's a natural feeling—we're pretty much wired with the need to be loved and accepted. God put it in our hearts so that we'd turn our eyes to Him, that we'd seek that acceptance in His eyes and loving arms. Because He is perfect and entirely loving beyond compare, God knows that a relationship with Him is the absolute greatest gift anyone could have. So He created us with that desire, that need to be loved.

Even when you have a relationship with God and you're getting that acceptance from Him, the temptation to get it elsewhere is still strong. You can be the strongest Christian around and still be tempted to trade away precious things so others will accept you. This happens to us in a lot of areas including the stands we've taken on dating and dress—two outward expressions of whom God has called us to be. When we choose to dress modestly and not date, we're taking up positions that make some people uncomfortable. That discomfort causes them to push on us to change, to be more like them, to be more acceptable. So we end up with a choice: Do we stick to our guns and risk people ripping on us and rejecting us? Or do we compromise on these issues for a comfy role in the crowd?

That temptation to conform for that comfort ends up wearing people down. Bit by bit, layer by layer, that temptation wears down a person's convictions until they've moved from being on fire for God, living out His word, to this mushy grey area of cutting corners or not standing up for what's right. We fight against that process all the time. We love being in a band. We want people

to enjoy hearing our music as much as we enjoy writing and performing it. We'll be honest—it's a great feeling to have people clap for something you've done. But if we chase that applause, that approval, as our only motivation, the drift from clear black and white to grey is underway. We've had people tell us we'd be more popular and sell more records and have bigger crowds at our concerts if we were less vocal about our God-given principles. We've shown up for performances and had people tell us, "Hey, don't talk so much about your beliefs; you'll freak people out." It's challenging.

We've prayed about this a lot as a family. Every day, that pull to conform drags on each one of us. Every day we have to go back to God and ask Him to help us in our commitment to Him. Because everyone needs His strength to stay away from the grey.

GREY

Grey's my favorite color
Black and white has never been my thing
I'll take my drink lukewarm now
Hot and cold is not the thing for me

Absolutes are hidden
I've buried my convictions

Chorus:
I cannot be blind no more
Numb to what I'm living for
Help me stop this compromise that justifies these lies
I need Your passion in this life

I don't want to impose
Who really needs to know what I believe
Cause no one likes rockin' boats
And who would care to see the way I see

So give me the fire, yeah
God give me Your fire
And raise this life higher

LET GO

Our dad grew up in a huge family—he's the sixth of fourteen kids (big round of applause to our grandmother, Teresa.) He used to tell us stories of how when one of them would get sick with one of the big childhood illnesses (measles, chicken pox, etc.) his parents would pile all of the kids into one room so they'd all get sick at the same time. In their opinion, they'd rather go through a week or two of many sick kids and get it over with than treating one sick kid after another as the germs went around. Can you imagine being in a room with eight or ten kids covered with red spots? Thankfully, our parents didn't do that to us. But, in some ways, some things in our lives are still contagious and we sometimes all come down with the same "bug."

When we were writing songs for our second album, we were sitting in our living room where we do most of our writing, feeling the pressure of yet another deadline. With just a week or two to go before we were headed back into the studio, it felt like the well had dried up. We were starting to journal and pray doubtful things, pretty much saying, "So, God have you turned off the song faucet up there? What's up?" As we sat there, the Great Physician (another name for Jesus—look it up) started to share His diagnosis with us. It turns out we were all suffering from some ridiculous case of spiritual amnesia. We had somehow managed to unlearn what He had so lovingly taught us over the past years, that He is entirely faithful, loving and sufficient (Does the phrase "more than enough" ring a bell?) We were so worried about meeting the expectations of our fans, the label, even each other, that we'd lost sight of His incredible track record of faithfulness and had jumped back into the driver's seat of our lives. Not only that, we were gripping the steering wheel so tight our knuckles were turning white.

That was an amazing breakthrough for us. It's a little embarrassing to have to keep relearning stuff God teaches us, but everyone deals

with that—it's human nature. Fortunately, God has a thing called grace that compensates for that. When He showed us that, we got a little spiritually red-faced for forgetting, but were also hugely relieved as the realization took hold. The process of letting go is a lifelong battle and the sickness of sin that flies around in the air is going to get us from time to time. Fortunately, in this big sick ward known as the world, we have company. We have our family and our friends to help us and a doctor who will heal us if we just listen to Him and trust Him enough to Let Go.

LET GO

Yeah I trust in You
I remember times You led me
This time it's bigger now
And I'm afraid You'll let me down

But how can I be certain?
Will You prove Yourself again?

Chorus:
'Cause I'm about to let go
And live what I believe
I can't do a thing now
But trust that You'll catch me
When I let go
When I let go

What is this doubt in me
Convincing me to fear the unknown
When all along You've shown
Your plans are better than my own

And I know I won't make it
If I do this all alone

I NEED YOU TO LOVE ME

Alyssa: Have you ever said something to a person who responded by looking at you like you'd just mumbled something in Swahili? That happened to me a while back in my own living room. I had been really seeking God's help on my tendency to choose hard work as the way to solve every problem, to prove to Him that I was worth His love. The harder I worked, the worse it hurt when things didn't go exactly as I'd planned. Louder and louder, I kept telling God the things I was planning to do for Him: "I'll clean myself up. I'll heed my calling. I'll earn your love."

During a personal reflection time in my bedroom, I was praying those phrases for the zillionth time when He interrupted me in an almost-but-not-quite-annoyed voice, "For once in your life, be quiet. Just stop talking. Just stop trying so hard. Take a break and allow yourself to rest. Let me love you just the way you are. I am, after all, God." That simple insight knocked me to my knees. I was completely humbled by His overwhelming love. Tears blurred my vision as I picked up my pen and journaled the phrase "I need you to love me." I wrote it again and then a third time, finally saying to God, "I'm done. I am finally ready to let you love me without trying to earn it."

I went downstairs where the other two-thirds of BarlowGirl were getting ready for a songwriting session and shared that with them. Becca, as the older sister, got it right away—very encouraging. When I turned to Lauren for her reaction, she was giving me "the look" I mentioned at the beginning of this chapter. She totally did not get the need to allow someone to love me. As the baby in the family, she had a totally different perspective on love than mine as middle child and Becca's as the oldest girl. Apparently, Lauren had always gotten what she needed in the love and attention department. "What do you mean, you don't

feel loved?" she asked. "We're all loved. I feel loved. You don't feel loved? What do you mean by earning love?" The fact that she was utterly confused by the concept only made us love her more. That's just the way she views life. It's the way God made her.

Since Lauren is a team player, she agreed to go along with the song (normally we don't do a song unless we're all 100% onboard with it in every respect) so we finished writing it together. And, in a very cool way, that disconnect allowed us to share things with each other about our own lives and fears that we might not have before.

Since the song was released, we have been amazed at how God has been using it in people's lives. It's amazing to think that, with the all-powerful God of the universe, it still comes down to each of us finally deciding to listen and let Him into our hearts before He'll come in and make our lives His own. So, if you're blessed to be like Lauren, feeling loved by those around you as well as God, realize how blessed you are. If you're like the rest of us, have the strength to cry out to Him, "I need you to love me."

I NEED YOU TO LOVE ME

Why, why are You still here with me
Didn't You see what I've done?
In my shame I want to run and hide myself
But it's here I see the truth
I don't deserve You

Chorus:
But I need You to love me, and I
I won't keep my heart from You this time
And I'll stop this pretending that I can
Somehow deserve what I already have
I need You to love me

I, I have wasted so much time
Pushing You away from me

I just never saw how You could cherish me
'Cause You're a God who has all things
And still You want me

Your love makes me forget what I have been
Your love makes me see who I really am
Your love makes me forget what I have been

PORCELAIN HEART

Do you ever hear people who are older, like maybe your parents or grandparents, talking about how things were better "in the old days?" To hear them tell it, things back then lasted longer—baby diapers were made of cloth, contact lenses were made of glass, cars were actually made of metal, stuff like that. These days, pretty much everything is disposable including diapers and contact lenses (which is great for quick cleanup). But, it also seems that the "disposable" factor has made things in general a little less special. Taking care of stuff isn't much of a priority because people know a) it's probably gonna break because it's made more cheaply and b) it won't kill us to buy a new one. That attitude seems to creep into other areas of life as well. Things that should be precious are merely seen as something to be bought and sold then misplaced or given away without a thought. In our generation, that attitude has even been adopted in terms of relationships. Marriages have become disposable, friendships evaporate over non-issues, and people bounce around multiple dating relationships without any regard to the consequences.

We know so many people who dove headfirst into the serial dating experience without realizing they were putting their hearts at risk. The way we see it, when you enter into a dating relationship, you're basically taking part in a practice marriage with all the same feelings and challenges (and, too often, the physical aspects as well). But dating lacks the "heart safeguards" of biblical marriage. In this pretend marriage world, there is no covenant, no binding commitment and the universal assumption that the relationship is temporary. A breakup (i.e. divorce) is pretty much the assumed, inevitable end of most dating arrangements. That system, in our throwaway world, leaves our generation littered with broken hearts.

In a prayer time a few years ago, Alyssa saw in her own heart

and mind, an image of a weeping girl kneeling on the floor of a
darkened room, trying and failing to piece together the broken
shards of a porcelain heart. When she shared this from her
journal, the sense of pain and loneliness and emptiness that girl
was feeling left a huge mark on us all. We're convinced that this
is what God sees as He looks into the lives of people everywhere,
people who smile on the outside and are absolutely shattered on
the inside. Our hearts are fragile and we're given only one, so we
need to guard them. The list of people we should give our hearts
to is a short one, starting with God. In this use-it-break-it-pitch-
it-and-buy-a-new-one world we live in, we need to protect our own
porcelain hearts and trust God for a love that lasts.

PORCELAIN HEART

Broken heart one more time
Pick yourself up, why even cry
Broken pieces in your hands
Wonder how you'll make it whole

Chorus:
You know, you pray
This can't be the way
You cry, you say
Something's gotta change
And mend this porcelain heart of mine

Someone said "A broken heart
Would sting at first then make you stronger"
You wonder why this pain remains
Were hearts made whole just to break

Creator only You take brokenness
And create it into beauty once again

TAKE ME AWAY

You know those airline commercials that ask the question "Need to get away?" About a year after the release of our first CD, our answer to that question was a huge YES! For almost two years, we'd been running a non-stop sprint of writing, rehearsing, recording, touring, performing and living the ministry God gave us. All of us were worn down to nothin' in every area, our minds, bodies and spirits. To be honest, we were also a little confused. We felt bad for feeling so stinkin' tired (and more than a little grouchy) from basically swimming in the amazing blessings God had been showering on us. Wasn't that supposed to energize us? We felt guilty for feeling like we needed a break from doing what we totally loved and, we believe, were made to do.

There is no question we needed physical rest, to sleep in our own beds and not be busy every minute of the day. But the tiredness went deeper. It was more than fatigue; we felt emptied out. So, we took advantage of a little-bit-longer-than-usual break on our touring schedule and headed back to the Chicago area, to the red brick home where we grew up. As we began to catch up on our sleep, we got back into our old-school routine of personal and family prayer times. As we dug back into the Bible and really focused on our journaling, we all realized that we had lost touch with the most important aspect of our entire lives--that quiet, intimate time with God. It had been way too long since we'd had one of those Psalm 23 moments, as in "He leads us beside still waters, He restores our soul."

It wasn't like we could look back and point to one date on the calendar and say, "That was where we decided to stop praying." Instead, that priority had been slowly leaking away. In our excitement to DO all the stuff God was setting before us, we had given bigger and bigger chunks of our lives to doing and less to dwelling in His presence. Being busy had overcome the sweet

intimacy that was the foundation of our relationship with God. Well, that negative trend had to stop. It was a "use it or lose it" moment. We had to use our time to pray or we would lose it (as in losing our minds and missing out on all the ministry opportunities that God still had for us.)

We all agreed to legitimately put prayer at the very tip-top of our personal and family lists, and give God the time He most definitely deserved. Sure, we also agreed to hold each other accountable on sleeping and exercising more, eating better and all that, but all of that had to take second place to hitting the big pause button of life, opening the Bible, and spending time with its author. The time spent beside those still waters is what replenishes us. Everybody needs a break from their crazy lives, but, in addition to saving up for a once-a-year trip to a far-away place, we all need to get away every day so that God can rest and replenish us.

TAKE ME AWAY

Pushing my way through these crowded streets
Trying not to be swept away
Fighting just to keep this crowd from
Hiding You another day

So maybe this time I'll find You
And maybe this time I'll push through
To see You today, today

Chorus:
Won't You take me away
Won't You take me away
'Cause I need some time to get away
Where only You could ever
Take me away, away, away
Too many days I've been distracted
Watched these crowds push You away
I'm so tired of feeling empty
Without You I waste these days

So maybe this time I'll find You
Just don't stop calling me to You
And I'll find my way today

PSALM 73 (MY GOD'S ENOUGH)

It is so easy to look around and think everyone has it better than you or me. We do that more than we should. To let you in on a little secret, we didn't have a ton of stuff growing up. This isn't a boo-hoo moment, but when your dad works on a church staff, you don't always have the big bucks piling up all over the house. (That's a fun idea—cutting paper dolls and snowflakes out of dollars—don't tell Uncle Sam we said that...) No matter how much you have of a favorite thing, there will always be someone who has one that's more expensive or newer or the so-much-more-perfect color. And, even if you somehow got that person's shiny treasure from them, you wouldn't be happy for long—you'd suddenly see an even better one in someone else's driveway or in their locker.

What is it about our world that makes stuff or awards feel so empty? Why do we care so much about what others think and have? Just about every time someone interviews us, they ask who our musical influences are. We name the Beatles, James Taylor and bands like dcTalk. But there was an amazing songwriter thousands of years ago—a guy named Asaph who wrote Psalm 73. He was a choir leader for King David, so he had a real close-up look at massive celebrity. He saw the way that people hurt each other, fighting to be the most popular, to have the most stuff, to put themselves above everyone else. Reading his words, you can really connect to his frustration with other people seeming to have everything better than him.

At the end of the psalm, though, it's like God flipped the light on and showed Asaph the truth. He shares that truth that the world and its little scoring system are meaningless when we consider God. Having gazed upon God's love and grace, the psalmist simply states that He is everything we need, the only thing we need. We need to hear that again and again—no matter how well we know that and burn it into our hearts with reflection and prayer, we still

live in the world and it tugs at us constantly.

Discontent lurks just around the corner, on the other side of that new shiny thing at the store. So, like all of our songs, God gave it to us because we needed to hear it first. But he also allowed us to share it with others because everyone struggles. By reminding ourselves of the insight from that original rock star, by storing up treasures on heaven instead of on earth, we are all able to rest in His grace.

PSALM 73 (My God's Enough)

I've had enough of living life for only me
And reaching just for the things that keep destroying me
So sick of envying the lives of so many I see
Somehow believing that they have what I need

Chorus:
My God's enough for me
This world has nothing I need
In this whole life I've seen
My God's enough, enough for me
I can't explain why I suffer though I live for You
Those who deny You they have it better than I do
Cover my eyes now so that my heart can finally see
That in the end only You mean anything

Who have I in heaven but You
Nothing I desire but You
My heart may fail but not You
You are mine forever

5 MINUTES OF FAME

Did you see that magician on TV a while back try to hold his breath underwater for nine minutes? Somehow they managed to stretch nine minutes of breathless panic into a two-hour show. People love that kind of stuff. As tough as that was for him, a few minutes really isn't a lot of time in the big picture. Even though we have a whole lifetime on this earth and eternity after that to consider, we end up choosing things—brief moments of acclaim or pleasure, winning an argument no matter what—whose benefits don't last at all.

When we choose things that run counter to the life God has called us to lead, the results can be devastating. We sisters are really blessed to have parents and friends who seek God and love us enough to set us straight. It doesn't always feel great when they're calling us on stuff, but that honesty and accountability help us grow as God's children. That doesn't mean we don't have arguments. It doesn't mean that we were three perfect angels when we were little. It does mean that God is still shaping us for the long haul with His unique set of tools including circumstances, trustworthy people and the inspiration of His word.

It's interesting to note that "selling out" isn't just a musician/performer thing. Every one of us has a chance to sell out in bad and good ways every day. "Selling out" literally implies a transaction, something being exchanged for something else. In the music world, angry fans accuse bands of trading their artistic integrity for a nice paycheck. But we each trade away a piece of ourselves when we choose to do wrong. If we have a chance to take a verbal shot at the new kid in school to help our own standing, we may enjoy the five minutes of fame that the laughter generates. But, we walk away from episodes like with a little less of our soul intact. Take advantage of enough of those opportunities, enjoy enough of those five minute chunks of fame and you'll end up with nothing

in your personal bank account—your integrity and character will be long gone.

So we encourage you to work that transaction in the other direction, staying humble (fame is overrated), loving others and encouraging them. That sort of exchange leaves us fuller than when we started. And, it sets us up for more than five minutes; it reminds us of and moves us toward an eternity of fame with God in heaven.

5 MINUTES OF FAME

It was a common story, yeah who cares that I changed?
Why are people freaking out?
Maybe I gave in more than I should, maybe I sold out
But the truth was I was really getting nowhere until
    I woke up and found
That morals can't take you up to the top your standards pull you down

Chorus:
Was it worth it what I gave away
For five minutes of fame
Minutes over no one knows my name
Or my minute of fame

I always said the thing that meant the most to me was
    my very integrity
Who would have thought I'd ever trade it all for popularity
'Cause the truth is though I've made it to the top I'm
    anything but satisfied
I gave up the only thing that mattered for this empty life

This time I'm saying no
This world will know what I believe in
I've lost enough to know
That life's too short to waste it

THOUGHTS OF YOU

We love love songs. We really do. There have been so many great ones in all the Broadway shows we've watched—"One Hand One Heart" from Westside Story, "On the Street Where You Live" from Hello Dolly, the list goes on. Let's not forget the great ones like Mr. Presley's "Love Me Tender" or even the Beatles' "P.S. I Love You." And that's just the songs from like a hundred years ago. (We're kidding—our mom and dad listened to that last one when they were younger.) Each of these songs illustrate that heartfelt ache to love and be loved that God built into us all so we'd hunger for Him.

Unfortunately, so many of us try to fill that void or satisfy that hunger with stuff that doesn't last. Whether you run after the approval of others or try to spend your way to wholeness, everything else falls short of God. He is the only one who genuinely completes us. Women go looking for Mr. Right without realizing that He has been around since before the beginning of time. When you finally get to know Him, when you really let God into the details of your life and hand your worries over to Him, your perspective starts to change. You go from a fear of not loving to the worry that you won't be able to love Him enough. Trust us, God has enough love for everyone.

When you reach that point of surrender and settle into that closer relationship with God, your life gets sweeter. Relationships get better because you're not depending on a friend or sibling or whomever to meet ALL your relational needs. Instead, God takes on that pressure for you (and has more love to give than any one person). Your work, whether you're doing it in a classroom or at a company, gets more enjoyable because your self-worth is no longer based on your ability to do it perfectly. The peace that flows out of knowing He loves all of us regardless is priceless.

We gotta admit that those peaceful seasons come and go. We

and everyone else we know seem to swing back and forth from humble reliance on God to the "I can do this myself" mode of isolation. As we ricochet between those two extremes, God never changes or moves away. Instead, He waits patiently for us to remember who we're living for so we'll run back into His arms. He always scoops up His kids when they ask. That's a God who deserves a love song, a song that we both sing and live out.

THOUGHTS OF YOU

Thoughts of You and how You changed me
Fill my mind
Without You where would I be

So even though I've tried to express my thanks
It never comes out how I hoped
I want to say so much more so with these simple words
I'll try

Chorus:
I love You
My heart is Yours, only Yours
I long to give You all of me
My everything, my everything

God I never could repay You
You gave everything
Without You where would I be

You still loved me even when I
Pushed You away
You stood there and waited
Till the day I'd return

What's Next?

As we reflect on where we've come from, what God has taught us and where we believe we're going, it's hard to believe He picked us for all of this. All along, we've tried to keep our priorities as God first, family second and music third. So He gets all the credit for anything good that has happened or will come our way in the future. God is the only one who can know what's next for us, but, if the past is any indication, it will include Him gently loving us, patiently teaching us and generously blessing us with the things that matter.

If you enjoy our music, we hope you'll continue to share it with others so that He can continue His work in every heart He touches. Oh, and pray for us too—chances are we'll continue making mistakes, losing sight of how He feels about us and needing Him more than ever.

About the Author

A proud BarlowUncle, Andrew Barlow lives in Austin, TX, with his wife and three great kids. For more information on his ministry, visit *www.apbcreative.com*.